*The* MONOCLE
*Travel Guide Series*

14

# Honolulu

For more information, please visit *gestalten.com*

———

Bibliographic information published by the Deutsche Nationalbibliothek: The Deutsche Nationalbibliothek lists this publication in the Deutsche National-bibliografie; detailed bibliographic data are available online at *dnb.d-nb.de*

Monocle editor in chief: *Tyler Brûlé*
Monocle editor: *Andrew Tuck*
Books editor: *Joe Pickard*
Guide editors: *Fiona Wilson, Kenji Hall*

———

Designed by *Monocle*
Proofreading by *Monocle*
Typeset in *Plantin & Helvetica*

———

Printed by *Offsetdruckerei Grammlich, Pliezhausen*

Made in Germany

Published by *Gestalten*, Berlin 2016
ISBN 978-3-89955-660-5

© Die Gestalten Verlag GmbH & Co. KG, Berlin 2016

**MIX**
Paper from responsible sources
FSC
www.fsc.org  **FSC® C011712**

This book was printed on paper certified by the FSC®

**Welcome**
—— Aloha

Hawaii has a reputation as a paradise of *sun, surf and ukulele tunes* and it's true all these elements abound in its capital. But there's also a less familiar side of *Honolulu* to discover, from its contemporary-art galleries and fine examples of mid-century architecture to a vibrant farm-to-table dining scene.

Our editors have crisscrossed the city and the wider island of O'ahu in search of these *pockets of dynamism*. This travel guide shines a spotlight on the standouts in their class: the fashion brands collaborating with Hawaiian manufacturers and artisans; the *chefs and distillers* championing homegrown produce; and the bars shunning drink umbrellas to focus on *inventive cocktails* served with hand-chiselled ice cubes.

We'll give you a rundown of everyday terms so you'll *know your 'poi' from your 'poke'*, show you where to find the best *slack-key guitar* tunes on vinyl, list our preferred hotels to hang our *'lauhala'* hats while in town and introduce the architects who designed the city's most *important landmarks*. And as no trip to Honolulu would be complete without time spent among Hawaii's bountiful natural assets, there's an entire section devoted to *watersports, hikes and day trips*.

This book is for anyone who wants to delve beyond the conventional clichés. Welcome to Honolulu. — (M)

# Contents
—— Navigating the city

Use the key below to help navigate the guide section by section.

096 —— 109
**Design and architecture**
Honolulu is home to a tropical modernist style that dates back to its transformation from backwater to travel hotspot. Taking in the work of Vladimir Ossipoff – whose buildings typify this style – plus the older delights of Chinatown and the more recent additions to the city, we point design aficionados in the right direction.

110 —— 121
**Sport and fitness**
You can't visit Honolulu and not check out the beaches, which is why we've rounded up all the best destinations for surfing, paddle-boarding, snorkelling or just relaxing. But don't let that be the limit of your activity: there are a host of walking, cycling and running trails to enjoy as well.

122 —— 129
**Walks**
One of the best ways to explore Honolulu is by foot so be sure to pack your walking shoes. Join us as we show you four ways to enjoy the city at a more leisurely pace.

130 —— 137
**Beyond the city**
Looking to explore a little further afield? Leave the city limits behind for the day and experience these out-of-town trips that we've tailored for your enjoyment.

138 —— 139
**Resources**
Local lingo, top tunes, tips for getting around town, what to do on rainy days and much more – all in one handy guide.

140 —— 141
**About Monocle**
Find out more about our global brand, from groundbreaking print, radio, online and film output through to our cafés and shops.

142 —— 143
**Acknowledgements**
The people who put this guide together: writers, photographers, researchers and all the rest.

144 —— 145
**Index**

# Map
## —— The city at a glance

Honolulu – the name means "sheltered harbour" in Hawaiian – sits on the southwestern corner of O'ahu island, nestled between the Pacific waters of Mamala Bay and Manoa's green volcanic slopes. The city's footprint isn't vast, although its sprawling network of highways can make it feel as though it is.

The oldest part of the city is near the port; the landmark Aloha Tower marks Honolulu's beginnings as a city of the sea. From here Chinatown – once a playground for sailors on leave, now a neighbourhood of colourful, independent businesses – and Downtown stretch inland. Wander south along the shore and you'll arrive at what is, for many, Honolulu's star draw, Waikiki. These waters are where modern surfing was born and are still where much of life in Honolulu unfolds. Head onwards and the built environment once again weaves itself into the tropical landscape – towards the iconic silhouette of the dormant Diamond Head volcano.

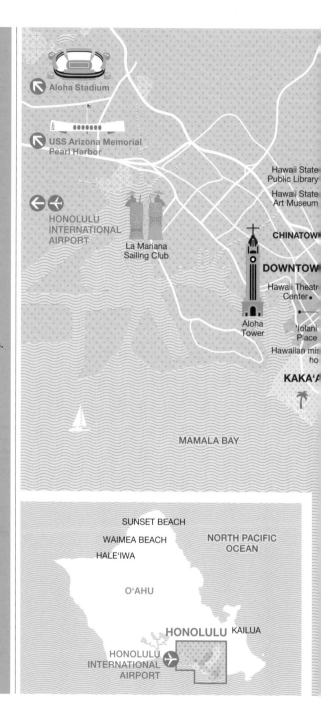

Aloha Stadium

USS Arizona Memorial
Pearl Harbor

HONOLULU
INTERNATIONAL
AIRPORT

La Mariana
Sailing Club

Hawaii State
Public Library

Hawaii State
Art Museum

CHINATOWN

DOWNTOWN

Hawaii Theatre
Center

'Iolani
Place

Hawaiian mis
ho

KAKA'A

Aloha
Tower

MAMALA BAY

SUNSET BEACH
WAIMEA BEACH
HALE'IWA

NORTH PACIFIC
OCEAN

O'AHU

HONOLULU  KAILUA

HONOLULU
INTERNATIONAL
AIRPORT

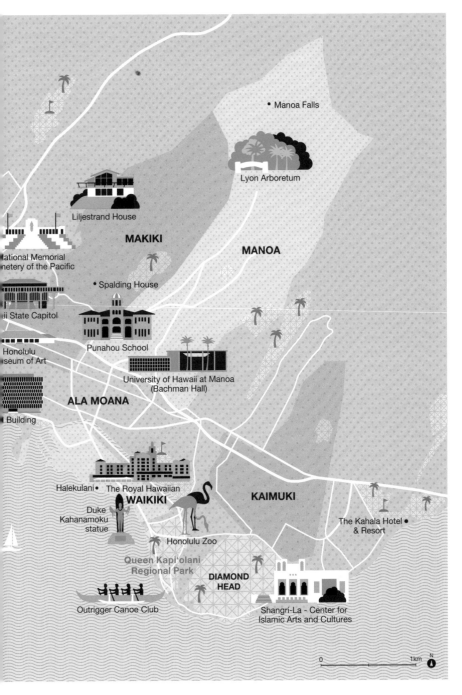
Manoa Falls

Lyon Arboretum

Liljestrand House

MAKIKI

MANOA

lational Memorial
netery of the Pacific

Spalding House

ii State Capitol

Honolulu
seum of Art

Punahou School

University of Hawaii at Manoa
(Bachman Hall)

ALA MOANA

Building

Halekulani • The Royal Hawaiian

Duke
Kahanamoku
statue

WAIKIKI

KAIMUKI

The Kahala Hotel •
& Resort

Honolulu Zoo

Queen Kapi'olani
Regional Park

DIAMOND
HEAD

Outrigger Canoe Club

Shangri-La - Center for
Islamic Arts and Cultures

0                    1km    N

# Need to know
—— Get to grips with the basics

While Hawaiians are welcoming folk, it's always handy to have a little insider information. From how to meet and greet to being prepared come rain or shine, these key tips, just like the Aloha Ambassadors, will point you in the right direction if this is your first visit to Honolulu.

## Handy gesture
The Shaka

Among Hawaiians, one hand gesture is indispensable: the Shaka. Made by extending the thumb and pinky, curling the three fingers in between and turning the back of the hand towards the recipient, the Shaka can mean "hello", "goodbye", "thank you", "take care" or any number of feel-good expressions. It's used both casually and formally: it can be seen in government photo ops and has become the de facto surfers' salute. One story traces its origin to an O'ahu man who lost his middle three fingers in a sugar-mill accident. In the 1960s and 1970s David "Lippy" Espinda, an entertainer, helped spread the gesture among the mainstream with his trademark phrase: "Shaka, brah".

## Talk the talk
Hawaiian

You will hear "aloha" and *mahalo* more than "hello" and "thank you". It's common for people to sprinkle their speech with Hawaiian, a language thought to have been brought here by Polynesian settlers centuries ago. Hawaiian relies on just 12 letters of the English alphabet and yet it can be richly descriptive: there are 225 words for the taro plant, and aloha is the equivalent of "hello" but means "breath of life". You will notice that the standard spelling for the state is Hawai'i, with the all-important okina: a glottal stop that indicates a pause. We've opted to use the English spelling for this guide but to pronounce the state name like a local, observe the pause: "huh-wah ee".

## So to speak
Hawaiian Pidgin English

*Da kine*? *Howzit*? *Shoots*? It takes a trained ear to follow the islands' creole: Hawaiian Pidgin English. Formally recognised by the US Census Bureau as a language in 2015, Pidgin was how immigrant labourers from China, Portugal, the Philippines and Japan communicated in the 19th and 20th centuries. About 600,000 of Hawaii's population of 1.4 million speaks Pidgin. As a group of University of Hawaii linguistics researchers wrote in a guide for teachers: "Ees da way plenny peepo in Hawaii tink."

*I'm both lost and lacking any idea as to how to use this*

## Standing guard
Aloha Ambassadors

Dressed in fluorescent green, the Aloha Ambassadors patrol the streets of Waikiki and help anyone in need. Launched in 2001 by the Waikiki Business Improvement District Association, this cheery band will give you directions, take your photo or even point you in the direction of the best fresh-fruit smoothie. And if they happen to be stumped by a question? They will radio the unanswered query into headquarters with the urgency of a military operation.

*Oh my, this is cordon bleu in a can*

## Spam alert
Eating

Spam musubi is the classic Hawaiian takeaway snack: a slice of Spam – usually fried in sweet soy sauce – on a small block of rice, all wrapped in dried seaweed. Hawaiians have the US military to thank for their love of the pink canned meat because for decades, dating back to the Second World War, it was served to soldiers stationed on the islands. The multitude of restaurants and shops selling Spam also partly accounts for the Hawaiians' huge appetite for the stuff: they eat nearly seven million cans every year, which amounts to about five cans per person and is the highest in the US on a per capita basis. Honolulu even has an annual Waikiki Spam Jam food-and-music festival.

## Cashing in
Money

It may be the most convenient place to change currency but a hotel won't give you the best exchange rate. In Waikiki try the banks or head to the DFS T Galleria at 330 Royal Hawaiian Avenue, which is open between 10.00 and 22.30; expect a queue.

## New leaf
Trees

Honolulu is a city of enormous trees. With their giant canopies, monkeypod and banyan trees offer protection from pelting rain or the heat of the sun; too bad these iconic varieties originated elsewhere. They are among the many plants that have crowded out native species since Captain James Cook set foot on Kauai in 1778 – a trend the city hopes to reverse. Since 2014 Honolulu has banned the use of any plants on city property that aren't indigenous to Hawaii or Polynesia. But legislators might want to think of an alternative to the city's official arboreal symbol: the decidedly non-native rainbow shower tree.

## Status symbol
Flag

The Hawaiian flag has an anomaly: a Union Jack in its top left-hand corner. This is a relic from the late 18th century when Hawaii was ruled by King Kamehameha I and the Union Jack was presented by a visiting British naval captain as a gift from King George III. After the war of 1812, Kamehameha commissioned a flag that incorporated the British flag. When Hawaii attained statehood in 1959, the flag became its official symbol with eight stripes, one for each of Hawaii's eight biggest islands. Today only the state flag – not the US flag – is flown over the royal residence 'Iolani Palace, reflecting the lingering resentment over the ousting of the monarchy in 1893.

## The name game
Language

*Haoles* can be *kama'aina* but *kama'aina* aren't necessarily *haoles*. Here's how it goes: *kama'aina* literally means "child of the land". Today it generally refers to Hawaii state residents; if you ask about the *kama'aina* discount in shops, be prepared to show ID. *Haole*, on the other hand, means "white person", but it used to refer to anything foreign. While the term long carried a negative association, now it is a neutral word that many Caucasian *kama'aina* even use to describe themselves.

## Right as rain
Weather

Honolulu may be renowned for its hot sunny days and laidback beaches but it's also a place that sees rainy days. Hawaii has two seasons – dry and wet – with the rainy season spanning October to April. During this period brief showers are not uncommon, even on seemingly clear days – particularly in December. It's even wetter at higher altitudes so if you're planning to hike in the mountains, don't forget to pack your wet-weather gear.

*In the absence of a figurehead, we have a bewildered owl*

# Hotels
## —— Tropical retreats

Cast your eyes inland from Waikiki's shoreline and you'll see a cityscape defined by a lush volcanic backdrop and a dense hotel strip that takes advantage of every square metre of beachfront. When tourism boomed in the 1960s, so did construction, turning a low-rise beach neighbourhood into an urban centre.

Most of the big chains are here and are very dependable. Waikiki has a good selection of its own historic hotels too: the serene Halekulani and the pink Royal Hawaiian are standouts. Outside of Waikiki, the options are more sparse. Honolulu's B&B selection is limited, as is mid-range accommodation. But openings such as the new Surfjack Hotel show that smaller-scale development is underway.

One point to note is how prices are calibrated in Honolulu. A hint of a sea view and the cost soars; a vista of the Diamond Head comes next and finally the city view. Decide which is most important to you beforehand.

① Halekulani, Waikiki
*Step back in time*

This historic beachfront hotel is, for many travellers, the best in Honolulu. The original hotel, Hau Tree, was opened in 1907. A decade later it was bought out and renamed Halekulani – House Befitting Heaven – and gradually expanded to include more cottages and a larger main building designed by one of Hawaii's great architects, Charles William Dickey.

Mitsui Fudosan bought the hotel in 1981 and remodelled it, replacing the old bungalows and restoring the Dickey building. The compact property now has 453 rooms set on two hectares and is a quiet oasis with serene decor. The service is thoughtful and friendly, a combination of Japanese attention to detail and Hawaiian aloha. Breakfast on the oceanfront terrace is an excellent way to start the day.
*2199 Kalia Road*
*+1 844 288 8022*
*halekulani.com*

MONOCLE COMMENT: Guests staying at Halekulani get complimentary entry to a number of cultural venues, including Doris Duke's Shangri-La, the Bernice Pauahi Bishop Museum, 'Iolani Palace and the Honolulu Museum of Art.

**②**

The Royal Hawaiian, Waikiki
*Pink palace*

It would be hard to think of Waikiki Beach without the pink portals of the Royal Hawaiian. The 400-room Spanish-Moorish-style hotel was built on 5.5 hectares of prime beachfront in 1927 and has stood the test of time while almost everything around it changed. The original building has a leafy garden, airy veranda and plenty of atmosphere. The "Pink Palace" features on aloha shirts, the Pacific Fleet came for R&R during the Second World War and Joan Didion wrote about staying here in 1969.

Today there are 528 rooms, including 33 suites and the newer Mailani Tower, which was revamped in 2015. The rooms have the requisite fine bed linen and fluffy bathrobes, while lovely touches include banana bread on arrival and toiletries from Hawaiian spa brand Malie Organics. Guests are welcomed with lei and can join in classes in ukulele, hula and yoga. There is also a pool with lavish cabanas, and surf and paddle-board lessons on the beach.

*2259 Kalakaua Avenue*
*+1 808 923 7311*
*royal-hawaiian.com*

MONOCLE COMMENT: Book an oceanfront room in the Mailani Tower. Higher rooms are more peaceful and have the grandest views.

*I'm converted: I'll never drink out of a dog bowl again*

③
The New Otani Kaimana Beach
Hotel, Waikiki
*Ocean-front setting*

This Japanese-owned 118-room
hotel on Honolulu's Gold Coast is
a tranquil retreat set slightly away
from the tourist bustle. Built in the
mid-1960s, it opens onto Kaimana
Beach (also known as Sans Souci),
a favourite swimming spot. The
rooms are simple but comfortable
and the views magnificent: from the
ocean-side balconies you can see
beyond the Waikiki Natatorium War
Memorial (*see page 108*). Tables at
the Hau Tree Lanai restaurant sit
beneath a famous hau (sea hibiscus)
tree (*see box, opposite*), right on the
relatively quiet shore. If you prefer to
go further afield, the famed Waikiki
Beach is a 15-minute walk away.
*2863 Kalakaua Avenue*
*+1 808 923 1555*
*kaimana.com*

MONOCLE COMMENT: Try the hotel's
other restaurant, Miyako, for
traditional Japanese food served
by kimono-clad waitresses.

*It's a gem*
—
'Kaimana'
means
'diamond' in
Hawaiian

### Music and hula in hotels

**01** Halekulani, Waikiki:
Every evening at the
House Without a Key
bar you can catch hula
performances by any one
of five former winners of
Miss Hawaii, with live
music from Pa'ahana,
Po'okela or the Sunset
Serenaders. Look for
Kanoe Miller, who has
danced there six nights
a week since 1977.
*halekulani.com*

**02** Outrigger Reef Waikiki
Beach Resort, Waikiki:
Top slack-key guitarists
feature at the Kani Ka
Pila Grille, with Weldon
Kekauoha, Cyril Pahinui
– the son of renowned
musician Gabby "Pops"
Pahinui – and Kawika
Kahiapo all in residence.
The bar's name is Hawaiian
for "to make music".
*outrigger.com*

**03** Moana Surfrider, Waikiki:
Among the artists who
perform in the hotel's
courtyard is Pomaika'i
Keawe Lyman. She is the
granddaughter of the late
"Aunty" Genoa Keawe,
one of Hawaii's most
treasured hula singers.
*moana-surfrider.com*

**04** Royal Hawaiian, Waikiki:
At the Mai Tai Bar, bands
including Kapala Duo, De
Lima Ohana and Eric Lee
play Hawaiian classics,
often sharing the stage
with dancers.
*royal-hawaiian.com*

**05** Hilton Hawaiian Village,
Waikiki: Nohelani Cypriano
and Jerry Santos, with his
band Olomana, have both
played their mellow sets
at the Tapa Bar for years.
The Tropics Bar & Grill has
hosted Grammy-nominated
vocalist Henry Kapono
Ka'aihue in the past.
*hiltonhawaiianvillage.com*

### Writer in residence

*Treasure Island* author Robert
Louis Stevenson often visited
O'ahu in the hope that the mild
climate would help his health.
One of his favoured spots
to relax and write was under
the hau tree in what would
become The New Otani's
garden. The hotel has a suite
named after him.

**④**

Hyatt Regency, Waikiki
*Cosy cabanas*

The reliable Hyatt Regency is set in the middle of the action on Kalakaua Avenue. The hotel has 1,230 recently renovated rooms with private *lanais* (covered patios) and – to please Japanese tourists – Toto washlets in the bathrooms.

The ocean-facing pool has private cabanas (with newspapers, drinks, fruit and ice lollies), and free chairs and towels are supplied for guests to take over the road to the beach.
*2424 Kalakaua Avenue*
*+1 808 923 1234*
*waikiki.regency.hyatt.com*

MONOCLE COMMENT: The hotel hosts a farmers' market every Tuesday and Thursday, from 16.00 to 20.00.

⑤
The Modern Honolulu, Waikiki
*Calm elegance*

The Modern Honolulu is a cut above the more conventional hotel options in Waikiki. The 353 rooms are spacious and the sparse white-and-beige colour scheme gives this glossy hotel a boutique feel despite its size. The hotel faces a small marina and has ocean views, while the nearest beach, Kahanamoku, is just a few minutes' walk away. For those who prefer to swim and lounge on-site there are two options: the Sunrise Pool or the elevated see-and-be-seen Sunset Pool lined with a manufactured beach and plenty of daybeds.
*1775 Ala Moana Boulevard*
*+1 808 943 5800*
*themodernhonolulu.com*

MONOCLE COMMENT: The hotel houses Morimoto Waikiki, opened in 2010 by chef Masaharu Morimoto. The restaurant is renowned for its sushi and fresh seafood dishes that combine elements of Japanese and Hawaiian cooking.

*Grand reception*
The lobby art is by surf hero Herbie Fletcher

**Touch of Japan**
—
The Breakers Hotel opened in 1954 and has 63 charming rooms with wooden louvre windows and shoji screens. Each Wednesday the owners, the Urasenke Foundation, hold a Japanese tea ceremony in the tea house next door.
*breakers-hawaii.com*

*I'm so engrossed in my travel guide that I haven't left this lounger*

**6**

The Kahala Hotel & Resort, Kahala
*Home to the stars*

Devotees of the grand 338-room
Kahala return to this resort hotel
year after year for its secluded
oceanfront location and old-school
charm. It's set in a smart residential
neighbourhood near the Waialae
Country Club and benefits from
privacy and discretion.

When the hotel opened as a
Hilton back in 1964, it quickly
became a favourite of Hollywood's
glitterati and came to epitomise
Honolulu in the sophisticated
1960s. Since then it has hosted
everyone from US presidents to
the Dalai Lama. No expense was
spared; the hotel even includes a
manmade lagoon – with dolphins.

The Kahala is not about
innovation. What guests come
back for are the cocktails and jazz
at The Veranda, a Kahala burger
on the terrace at the Plumeria
Beach House and *ahi poke*
(raw-tuna salad, see page 33) at
fusion restaurant Hoku's.
*5000 Kahala Avenue*
*+1 808 739 8888*
*kahalaresort.com*

MONOCLE COMMENT: Ocean-view
rooms are first choice but the
outlook from the back, over the
Ko'olau Mountains, is more scenic
than from other hotels in the city.

(7)
Lotus Honolulu, Diamond Head
*Give peace a chance*

Lotus Honolulu has what most Waikiki hotels lack: quiet surroundings. Located next to Queen Kapi'olani Regional Park, a 15-minute walk from the Waikiki strip, it boasts 51 spacious, well-appointed rooms, each with a daybed, private balcony and tropical-flower-themed decor. The attentive service and easygoing atmosphere attract regulars who stay for months at a time.
*2885 Kalakaua Avenue*
*+1 808 922 1700*
*lotushonoluluhotel.com*

MONOCLE COMMENT: There's no pool but the health-conscious might start the day with a swim at Kaimana Beach or a run at Diamond Head.

My plants love listening to 'The Monocle Daily'

**Elegant bloom**
The decor at the Lotus is tastefully tropical

Ⓧ
Waikiki Parc Hotel, Waikiki
*Action-packed offering*

Situated across the street from its
grander sister property, Halekulani,
Waikiki Parc offers 297 rooms
that are large and comfortable in a
contemporary style. Where "city-
view" rooms can sometimes signify
a downgrade in other Waikiki hotels
that's not the case here: the vista of
Honolulu, as it stretches up into the
green volcanic hills from Waikiki Parc,
is charming, especially at night.

There is a rooftop pool and a
range of activities on offer, from
wine-tastings every Friday to early-
morning paddle-board lessons. Nobu
Waikiki, serving innovative Japanese
cuisine, is on the ground floor.
*2233 Helumoa Road*
*+1 808 921 7272*
*waikikiparc.com*

MONOCLE COMMENT: Guests can
sign for food and drinks at the five-
star Halekulani, which is just a few
steps away. Both hotels are owned
by the same Japanese company,
Mitsui Fudosan.

Ⓧ
Moana Surfrider, Waikiki
*The grande dame*

Moana Surfrider has a proud
history. Hailed as Waikiki's first
hotel, the original 1901 building has
the look of a wooden wedding cake
and was designed by US architect
Oliver G Traphagen. UK crime
writer Agatha Christie stayed here
in 1922 and legendary Olympic
swimmer Duke Kahanamoku
frolicked on its private beach. It
was inscribed on the US National
Register of Historic Places in 1972.

The hotel entrance is on Kalakaua
Avenue, Waikiki's main thoroughfare,
and the three buildings stretch back
to the beach. Its 791 rooms are
simple and comfortable, although
the modern exteriors don't quite
live up to the venerable days of old.
Today it is one of the most popular
wedding venues in Hawaii, evidenced
by the many blushing brides and
grooms striking a pose for their
photographers in its wood-panelled
lobby. Tourists throng here, dropping
in for a peek and a drink at its bar.
*2365 Kalakaua Avenue*
*+1 808 922 3111*
*moana-surfrider.com*

MONOCLE COMMENT: The service at
the outdoor pool is second to none:
staff will offer you an extra towel on
your way to the water or keep you
abreast of the latest weather forecast.

**Branching out**
———

In the centre of Moana
Surfrider's courtyard is a 23-
metre tall banyan tree (*pictured
below*). It was planted in 1904
by the US Department of
Agriculture Experiment Station
and has become a Honolulu
landmark. In 1979 it was
added to Hawaii's Exceptional
Tree list.

Retro update
—
The decor
harks back to
1960s Hawaii

**⑩**
Surfjack Hotel & Swim Club, Waikiki
*Arty retreat*

Opened in 2016 in a 1960s building,
the Surfjack Hotel & Swim Club
is part of a new breed of forward-
thinking hotels. It's also a great
example of Hawaii's rustic charm.
The 112 rooms – half of them suites
– have reed ceilings, custom-made
tiles and headboards covered with
vintage textiles. The hotel also
showcases the work of Hawaiian
artists, giving it a vibrant ambience.
    The restaurant, Mahina & Sun's,
run by renowned island chef Ed
Kenney, serves dishes made with
organic ingredients. Exotic cocktails
and a specially blended coffee called
Hale 412, roasted exclusively for
The Surfjack, are also on offer.
*412 Lewers Street*
*+1 808 923 8882*
*surfjack.com*

MONOCLE COMMENT: The hotel has
a "director of experience" who can
connect visitors to artists, musicians
and makers on O'ahu or arrange an
architecture tour of the island.

# Food and drink
—— Island dining

Traditional Hawaiian cuisine is rooted in the land, as evidenced by typical dishes such as *kalua* pig (pork roasted in a pit oven), *laulau* (pork slow-cooked in taro leaf) and *poi* (a starch staple made from pounded taro). But food today in Honolulu is more of a hodgepodge, reflecting the tastes of the waves of immigrants who have come to these islands from Portugal, China, Japan, South Korea, Vietnam, the Philippines and elsewhere over more than two centuries.

Unfamiliar terms abound – *opakapaka* for snapper, *limu* for algae, *shoyu* for soy sauce – but don't be intimidated. It's a good time for dining in Honolulu: pioneering chefs such as Ed Kenney, Andrew Le, Jesse Cruz, Brian Chan and others are reinventing local fare at restaurants, plate-lunch counters, farmers' markets and food trucks. In making it possible to eat meat, fish, vegetables and fruit grown or caught in and around Hawaii, these chefs are focusing attention on the islands' producers as never before.

**Restaurants**
Top tables

①
Pioneer Saloon, Diamond Head
*Japanese twist*

Owner-chef Nori Sakamoto's creations are a Japanese take on the Hawaiian plate-lunch. The ingredients might be recognisable but perhaps not the cooking method: *ahi* (tuna) or scallops breaded and fried, rib-eye steak bowl and chicken cooked in *shio-koji*, an umami-rich seasoning. After your meal, walk next door to Kenta Nagano's Monsarrat Shave Ice, where the syrups are made with natural ingredients.
*3046 Monsarrat Avenue*
*+ 1 808 732 4001*

② **Kan Zaman, Chinatown**
*Spice of life*

Owner-chefs Kamal Jemmari, who is from Marrakech, and Youssef Dakroub, from Beirut, met while running their own taco trucks in Honolulu. They joined forces in 2013 and now cook delicious, unfussy Moroccan and Lebanese meals with cinnamon, ginger, saffron, cumin and other spices mixed by Jemmari's mother. Kan Zaman ("once upon a time" in Arabic) has cheerful vermilion and turquoise walls and the extensive menu includes tabbouleh, *warak enab* (stuffed grape leaves), shawarmas, tagines and couscous dishes.
*1028 Nuuanu Avenue*
*+ 1 808 554 3847*
*kanzamanhawaii.com*

**Global influence**
——
Bills mixes local produce and world flavours

③ **Bills, Waikiki**
*Relaxed Aussie influence*

Bill Granger's laidback Aussie style works a treat in Honolulu. Located near the ocean, Bills features a beach bar on its ground floor and a restaurant upstairs. The sun-bleached interior is a welcome departure from Waikiki's more generic offerings.

Opening at 07.00 with a breakfast menu, the service continues into lunch and dinner. Fresh produce sourced nearby infuses a menu that takes inspiration from Japan, Vietnam, South Korea and beyond: courgette fritters with tahini yoghurt, yellowfish curry with butternut squash, kimchee fried rice and pizza.
*280 Beachwalk Avenue*
*+ 1 808 922 1500*
*billshawaii.com*

## Japanese restaurants

**01** Nanzan GiroGiro, Ala
Moana: Chef Yoshihiro
Matsumoto uses only the
freshest produce for his
multi-course *kaiseki* (Japan's
version of haute cuisine).
+1 808 524 0141

**02** Yohei Sushi, Kalihi-
Palama: This restaurant
has attracted a loyal
following over the past
20 years. The *omakase*
course (the chef picks it)
is a winner.
+1 808 841 3773

**03** Menya Musashi, Ala
Moana: This Tokyo-based
ramen-noodle specialist
opened its first US shop
here in 2013.
*musashiramen.weebly.com*

**04** Inaba, McCully-Moʻiliʻili:
Regulars rave about the
handmade buckwheat
soba noodles. But
everything here, from
tempura to udon,
is authentic.
*inabahonolulu.com*

**05** Sushi Izakaya Gaku, Ala
Moana: Chef Manabu
Kikuchi allows only the
best fish to make it onto
his sushi menu.
+1 808 589 1329

**06** Sushi Sasabune, Ala
Moana: Expect properly
served sushi in this low-key
restaurant specialising in
13-course *omakase*.
+1 808 947 3800

### Taste of Japan

Food from Okinawa, Japan's
southernmost region, is the
speciality at Izakaya Naru.
Expect bold flavours in such
dishes as *goya champuru* (stir-
fried bittermelon) and *shoyu*
pork belly. Try the *awamori* too,
an Okinawan distilled liquor.
*naru-honolulu.com*

④
Dim-sum restaurants, Chinatown
*Traditional flavour*

Honolulu has one of the oldest
Chinatowns in the US and a
culinary pedigree to match.
Along the river outside Fook Lam
Restaurant, men gather at tables
to play board games. Inside, the
pace is more frenetic. Be sure to
grab the cucumber in special sauce
and the Shanghai soup dumplings
(*xiao long bao*).

Like Fook Lam, Legend Seafood
Restaurant is in the Chinatown
Cultural Plaza. It serves dim sum
until 14.00; don't miss the prawn
dumplings and fried taro puffs. At
Mei Sum (*pictured*) on Nuuanu
Avenue, the dim sum, including
garlic soft-shell crab, is served
until 21.00.
*Fook Lam Restaurant:*
*100 North Beretania Street*
*+1 808 523 9168*
*Legend Seafood Restaurant:*
*100 North Beretania Street*
*+1 808 532 1868*
*Mei Sum: 1170 Nuuanu Avenue*
*+1 808 531 3268*

*Ah. The
dumplings
diet isn't
working*

 ⑤
Dew Drop Inn, Chinatown
*Neighbourhood treasure*

This intimate restaurant celebrates the food of Taiwan, where its owner Charlie Tsai hails from, and northern China. Customers pile in for dishes such as *xiao bing* (sesame bread pockets stuffed with tofu, pork or chicken). It's proudly MSG-free and diners can bring their own alcohol.
*1088 South Beretania Street*
*+ 1 808 526 9522*
*dewdropinnhawaii.com*

⑥
Char Hung Sut, Chinatown
*Bigger is better*

This busy shop on Pauahi Street is takeaway only. Entering through either door you will find women working dough on a large metal table and someone behind the register ready to pack you a box of pork hash, half-moon dumplings, or *manapua* (steamed buns, also known as *char siu bao*). Bat Moi Kam Mau, who opened Char Hung Sut in 1945 as a teahouse that served dim sum, claims that the business was the first to have taken the smaller Chinese *char siu bao* and supersized them for local consumption. Bring cash: cards are not accepted.
*64 North Pauahi Street*
*+ 1 808 538 3335*
*charhungsutrestaurant.com*

 ⑦
Mud Hen Water, Kaimuki
*Hawaiian nostalgia*

Chef Ed Kenney is a prominent figure on the Honolulu restaurant scene: he also runs Town (see *page 30*) and Kaimuki Superette (see *page 33*). Mud Hen Water focuses on showcasing the Hawaiian cuisine he grew up with.

The *crudité* features hummus and crunchy *kukui* (candlenut) chips; octopus in a soupy stew of *lu'au* (taro) leaves with nuts, herbs and spices; and *opah* (moonfish) wrapped in banana leaves and cooked over coals. Much of the produce is organic and Kenney's farm-to-table ethos extends to the cocktails too.
*3452 Waialae Avenue*
*+ 1 808 737 6000*
*mudhenwater.com*

**Must-try**

Saimin from Shige's Saimin Stand, Wahiawa

Among Hawaiians, *saimin* – noodles in a light, savoury broth – can generate the kinds of superlatives common among ramen fans. The best *saimin* is made by family-run hole-in-the-wall shops that have been around for decades. You'll find Ross Shigeoka's spot, which he opened in 1990, on the road from Honolulu to the North Shore. He makes his noodles and prawn-and-beef soup from scratch.
*+1 808 621 3621*

(8)
Grondin French-Latin Kitchen, Chinatown
*Multicultural club*

The menu is an homage to co-owners Jenny Grondin's French heritage and David Segarra's Ecuadorian roots. Croque madame and cassoulet sit alongside prawn ceviche, *chuleta* (pork-loin chop) and duck-confit crêpes mole negro.

Grondin and Segarra worked in restaurants in New York before moving to Hawaii for a better quality of life. Their kitchen, led by chef Andrew Pressler, opens for dinner daily and also serves lunch on weekdays and brunch on weekends.
*62 North Hotel Street*
*+1 808 566 6768*
*grondinhi.com*

9
Town, Kaimuki
*Produce proponent*

Chef Ed Kenney's dedication to supporting Hawaiian farmers can be seen in his approach to Italian-style dishes. The menu at Town changes daily according to what ingredients are available but may include mahi mahi with vegetables and *limu* (algae), *pa'i'ai* (mashed taro root) with fennel and mackerel or *sugo di cinghiale* (wild boar) pasta.

Opened in 2005, Town was the first of Kenney's food ventures in Kaimuki (*see pages 29 and 33*) and its success established his reputation as a trailblazer among Hawaiian chefs.
*3435 Waialae Avenue*
*+1 808 735 5900*
*townkaimuki.com*

⑩
Artizen by MW, Downtown
*Food for art's sake*

Visiting the Hawaii State Art
Museum is an even more pleasant
experience now that Artizen by
MW is serving food downstairs
on weekdays. Run by owner-chefs
Michelle Karr-Ueoka and Wade
Ueoka, it opens at 07.30 and has
a menu that's great for carb-
loading. For lunch try the tuna
and basil pesto sandwich, the
miso-soy-braised short ribs or
the spicy South Korean pork bowl.
There's also an assortment of
salads from produce grown
around Hawaii and takeaway
bento meals.
*250 South Hotel Street*
*+1 808 524 0499*
*artizenbymw.com*

⑪
Livestock Tavern, Downtown
*Meat-centric meals*

Co-owners and Honolulu natives
Dusty Grable and chef Jesse Cruz
opened Livestock Tavern in October
2014, turning a former dive bar into
one of the city's most acclaimed
dining spots. The food is seasonal and
nourishing and the service excellent.
The supper menu features a slew of
small plates for sharing and mains
of osso buco, pork cheeks and a
stuffed herb-roasted chicken that's
been brined overnight. Livestock is
near the pair's first restaurant, Lucky
Belly (*see page 32*); its inviting, dimly
lit interior is the work of Grable's
designer wife Elyse.
*49 North Hotel Street*
*+1 808 537 2577*
*livestocktavern.com*

⑫
Encore Saloon, Chinatown
*Latin flavours*

It might seem strange to recommend
Mexican street-style food in
Chinatown but if you don't try
Encore Saloon's tacos (spit-roasted
pork, slow-braised beef) you will
have missed out.
    Found in the Encore Saloon
Building (built in 1886), the
restaurant is a more spacious
version of the hole-in-the-wall
*taqueria* that restaurateur Danny
Ka'aiali'i ran for years in the
Kaka'ako area, to widespread
acclaim. On weekends Encore
Saloon opens for brunch, with
Mexican-influenced items such as
*horchata* (rice milk) French toast.
*2 North Hotel Street*
*encoresaloon.com*

### O'ahu specialities

**01**  Hank's Haute Dogs,
Kaka'ako: Hankering
for a rabbit-sausage
hot dog served with
mushrooms and a
Dijon-truffle cheese
sauce? Hank's Haute
Dogs is the place to
go for exotic frankfurters.
*hankshautedogs.com*

**02**  Senia, Downtown:
Chefs Chris Kajioka
and Anthony Rush
and manager Katherine
Rush have teamed up
for this restaurant that
showcases modern cuisine
created with Hawaiian-
grown ingredients.
*restaurantsenia.com*

**03**  Musubi Café Iyasume,
Waikiki: Iyasume
makes what is widely
considered to be the
tastiest Spam musubi:
premium Nanatsuboshi
rice from Hokkaido
topped with grilled
Spam and bound with
a belt of dried seaweed
*tonsuke.com/eomusubiya*

**Ono Hawaiian Foods, Kapahulu**
*Word of mouth*

"Ono" means delicious in Hawaiian and it's an apt description for this small family-run restaurant, that the late Sueko Miyagi Oh Young opened in 1960. Traditional meals that gained popularity in the mid-20th century are all represented – *kalua pig* (slow-cooked pork), *pipikaula* (dried salted beef), *lomi lomi salmon* (raw salmon and tomato salad) and *poi* (taro root) – and they arrive in heaped portions on plastic plates to share.

There's nothing fancy about the decor but the food is reliably excellent and filling. Cash only.
*726 Kapahulu Avenue*
*+1 808 737 2275*
*onohawaiianfoods.com*

**The Pig & the Lady, Chinatown**
*Vietnamese street food*

This restaurant was opened in 2013 by Honolulu-born chef and co-owner Andrew Le. Since then he has given diners a crash course in Vietnamese pho and *banh mi* sandwiches, seasonal Hawaiian comfort food and his own concoctions, such as a brisket sandwich with pho dipping sauce.

Le's elder brother Alex runs the restaurant's food stalls at various farmers' markets (including Kailua and KCC markets, see page 38), where the *canh chua chay* vegetable sour noodle-soup is always a crowd-pleaser.
*83 North King Street*
*+1 808 585 8255*
*thepigandthelady.com*

**Olive Tree Café, Kahala**
*Greece is the word*

Head here for Honolulu's tastiest no-frills Greek food. The wonderfully smoky baba ganoush and *dolmadakia* (stuffed vine leaves) are a good place to start. We also recommend the grilled fish souvlaki featuring the day's catch, covered in tzatziki and wrapped in a warm pita (there's also grilled kebabs of lamb or chicken).

Alcoholic drinks are not served on the premises but you can bring your own or stop by at Oliver, the wine shop next door that's run by the same owners.
*4614 Kilauea Avenue*
*+1 808 737 0303*

**Lucky Belly, Chinatown**
*Late-night noodles*

This ramen restaurant was the first venture from Dusty Grable and Jesse Cruz (they also own Livestock Tavern, see page 31) and it's a popular choice for late-night fare. The signature dish, Belly Bowl, is a savoury treat: pork belly, smoked bacon and sausage in a pork broth that's simmered for hours. The rest of the menu is just as original: a mishmash of Japanese, South Korean, Chinese and Vietnamese flavours. Closing time is midnight but takeout is available until 02.30 from Thursday to Saturday.
*50 North Hotel Street*
*+1 808 531 1888*
*luckybelly.com*

*Eating pork belly is thirsty work*

(17)

### Kaimuki Superette, Kaimuki
*Market values*

The name of this small deli diner
implies a mini-mart, which is ideal
because many of the ingredients in
the dishes can be purchased to take
home. It caters to the breakfast and
lunch crowds and was opened by
Ed and Kristen Kenney and Dave
Caldiero in 2015; a few doors down
you'll find sister restaurants Mud
Hen Water (*see page 29*) and Town
(*see page 30*). Try the chia-seed
pudding and the sausage sandwich
with choi sum. Supporting Hawaiian
farmers is an aim: many of the
goods, such as the pork, honey and
coffee beans, are locally produced.
*3458 Waialae Avenue*
*+1 808 734 7800*
*kaimukisuperette.com*

**Must-try**
Poke from Alicia's Market,
Kalihi
*Poke* means to cut into pieces
and in a culinary sense it refers
to raw tuna that's cubed,
marinated and piled on rice
(smoked octopus and prawn
versions are also common).
Alicia's Market is our *poke* pick:
only the freshest tuna is used.
*aliciasmarket.com*

**Food terms in
Hawaii**
——
**Ahi:** tuna
**Haupia:** coconut pudding
**Kalo:** taro
**Limu:** seaweed or algae
**Ono:** wahoo (fish)
**Opakapaka:** snapper
**Pipikaula:** dried beef
**Pupu:** appetiser
**Shoyu:** soy sauce
**Tako:** octopus

(18)

### Tonkatsu Ginza Bairin, Waikiki
*Tonkatsu heaven*

This is the Honolulu outpost of
Bairin, a Tokyo institution since
1927. The speciality is *tonkatsu*:
tenderised pork breaded and fried.
The *hito-kuchi* (bite-sized) cutlet and
sweet brown sauce made with apples
were the inventions of Ginza Bairin
founder Nobukatsu Shibuya.
*255 Beach Walk*
*+1 808 926 8082*
*pj-partners.com/bairin*

⑲
Ono Seafood, Kapahulu
*Peak demand*

At the back of the American Savings Bank car park is the takeaway-only counter where founder Judy Sakuma has been selling her bowls of tuna and octopus *poke* (*see page 33*) and sashimi plates since 1995. Sakuma gets her premium-grade fish every morning at Honolulu's fish auction (*see page 38*) and every dish is made to order.

The queue stretches out the door during lunchtime. Her *poke*, served over white or brown rice, comes with algae, *kukui* (candlenut), chilli pepper, sesame and a "savoury secret *shoyu*" (soy sauce), the ingredients for which she keeps close to her chest.
*747 Kapahulu Avenue*
*+ 1 808 732 4806*

**Must-try**
Poi and pa'i'ai
This nutritious paste made from pounded taro root was a culinary staple brought to Hawaii by early Polynesian settlers. Recently *poi*, along with the hand-crushed variety known as *pa'i'ai*, has made a comeback in restaurants run by chefs keen to promote homegrown produce and lessen the use of imported goods. *Poi*'s attraction is its versatility: it can be grilled, deep-fried or made into a batter or puree.
*townkaimuki.com*

**Breakfast and lunch**
Daytime bites

❶
Scratch Kitchen & Bake Shop, Chinatown
*Spice of life*

You could eat for days at Brian Chan's café without repeating your order. His menu is influenced by Latin American, Mediterranean and Southern cooking, with such creations as Creole shrimp and grits and a chorizo breakfast burrito.
*1030 Smith Street*
*+ 1 808 536 1669*
*scratch-hawaii.com*

②
Banán, Diamond Head
*Fruity goodness*

While travelling, four high-school friends – Matt, Zak, Luke and Galen – came across dairy-free ice cream that used pulped bananas instead of milk, cream and sugar. Upon returning home to Honolulu they pooled their savings, bought a food truck and have been creating their creamy iced-banana-and-fruit bowls since 2014. Banán uses only Hawaii-grown bananas, composts its waste and sends peels to a pig farmer for feed. They mix in açaí, spirulina, mint, ginger, passion fruit and mango for a perfect post-workout treat.
*3212 Monsarrat Avenue*
*+ 1 808 392 8862*
*bananbowls.com*

**③**

Wailana Coffee House, Waikiki
*Comfort food*

When Francis Tom moved his business from Honolulu Zoo to its current location on Ala Moana Boulevard in 1958, Waikiki was a backwater. Over time Tom's business evolved from a drive-in to a sit-down counter and a self-service canteen. Today it's a 250-seat, 24-hour diner and bar that's run by his three children, Kenton, Joanna and Malcolm. The counter and booth seats, flower-print carpet and brass lamps are comfortably dated and its menu caters to the masses: all-you-can-eat pancakes, New York steaks and a meatloaf that debuted in 1969.
*1860 Ala Moana Boulevard*
*+1 808 955 1764*

Start-up food
—
Big breakfasts are a Waikiki staple

**Light refreshment**
—
Goofy Café & Dine, a haven of fresh Hawaiian produce, has been an antidote to Honolulu's greasy breakfast options since 2013. The daily green veggie juice is refreshing and you can order a spiked sugarcane sour cocktail during lunch and dinner (or both).
*goofy-honolulu.com*

Coffee: check. Next on the agenda: pancakes

Shaka Pressed Juice, Diamond Head
*Juice on the loose*

Co-owners Juri and Keegan Edwards opened their takeaway cold-pressed juice shop in 2015 along a popular running route. They turn organic produce from Hawaii and the mainland into more than a dozen drinks and use no artificial additives. Shaka also serves salads and granola.
*3118 Monsarrat Avenue*
*+1 808 200 0921*
*shakapressedjuice.com*

**6**

Eggs'n'Things, Waikiki
*Breakfast club*

At this breakfast and brunch institution the platters of pancakes and waffles are barely visible beneath the peaks of cream. Jerry and Jan Fukunaga first set up shop in 1974 and now have three locations, each of which commonly boasts queues snaking around the block (the wait for a table can stretch to an hour or more). The crab cake Benedict is a treat, as are the freshly pressed fruit juices. Empty your plate and you won't need to eat for the rest of the day.
*343 Saratoga Road*
*+1 808 926 3447*
*eggsnthings.com*

**4**

Mission Social Hall and Café, Downtown
*True calling*

Mark Noguchi brings a Hawaiian perspective to his cooking. He grew up in Manoa and spent several years performing with Halau O Kekuhi, a traditional hula ensemble. At Mission Social Hall and Café (inside the cluster of early mission houses in the city centre), his lunch menu offers favourites such as *lu'au* stew with pork and taro leaves. It's open for lunch from Tuesday to Saturday, 11.00 to 14.00, and hosts a *pau hana* (after-work) get-together on the third Wednesday of every month from 17.00 to 19.00.
*553 South King Street*
*+1 808 447 3913*
*missionhouses.org*

I shouldn't have eaten those pancakes

Koko Head Café, Kaimuki
*Out to brunch*

Owner-chef Lee Anne Wong raised
the bar for brunch in Hawaii when
she opened this café in 2013. Her
wildly original menu features
unforgettable cornflake French
toast, miso-and-smoked-pork
omelette and muffins made with
black sesame and yuzu citrus.

Wong, a New York native, was
a *Top Chef* contestant and later
a producer on the popular TV
show. Don't miss her versions of
Hawaiian standards such as the
Koko Moco, a riff on the classic
meat, egg, rice and gravy dish
(*see bottom, left*).
*1145C 12th Avenue*
*+ 1 808 732 8920*
*kokoheadcafe.com*

⑦
Rainbow Drive-In, Kapahulu
*Going loco*

Rainbow Drive-In has been serving
heaping plates of *loco moco* (*see
below*), *shoyu* chicken (soy-sauce
chicken) and pork long rice since
1961 and is a neighbourhood
landmark thanks to its neon sign.
It was opened by Seiju and Ayako
Ifuku (Seiju was an army chef
during the Second World War) and
is treasured for its straightforward
offering: rice, salad and a selection
of substantial mains such as
breaded pork, mahi mahi or
boneless chicken, with the option
to drown the lot in gravy. It's open
for breakfast, lunch and dinner.
*3308 Kanaina Avenue*
*+ 1 808 737 0177*
*rainbowdrivein.com*

⑩
Liliha Bakery, Liliha
*Step back in time*

With its long counter, vinyl-
upholstered stools, generous
portions and 24-hour service, Liliha
Bakery is the classic greasy spoon;
regulars go for waffles and pancakes.
The bakery sells thousands of coco
puffs (cream puffs with cocoa
custard) every day but the Hawaiian
desserts – *dobash*, *chantilly* and
*haupia* – are a big draw too. Opened
in 1950 by Ray and Koo Takakuwa,
Liliha moved to its current location
11 years later. In 2008, Peter Kim
became the new owner but he has
wisely left Liliha mostly unchanged.
Closed Mondays.
*515 North Kuakini Street*
*+ 1 808 531 1651*
*lilihabakeryhawaii.com*

⑧
Bogart's Cafe, Diamond Head
*Bagels and more*

Mornings are when Bogart's is at
its busiest. To avoid the queue, get
there early – opening time is 06.00
– for the popular breakfast bagels
(there are 13 types) that come
with egg, jack cheese and cheddar
cheese, spinach and tomato.

Since Maria Barnette converted
a shave ice and ice-cream shop
into her café in 2000, she has made
eggs a speciality: the omelettes
and variations on eggs Benedict
are excellent. Anyone craving
fresh fruit can find plenty of it
in the açaí bowls, Belgian waffles
and pancakes.
*3045 Monsarrat Avenue*
*+ 1 808 739 0999*
*bogartshawaii.com*

**Must-try**
Loco moco from Morning
Glass Coffee + Café, Manoa
This artery-clogging take on
the hamburger – a meat patty
with gravy and an egg on rice
– is thought to have been
invented in the late 1940s.
Morning Glass Coffee + Café's
version uses beef from grass-
fed cows and a ranchero sauce.
*morningglasscoffee.com*

## Food markets
Bountiful Honolulu

**②**
Kailua Farmers' Market, Kailua
*Spice of life*

On Thursdays from 17.00 to 19.30 head to Kailua on O'ahu's southeastern side to peruse the vibrant food stalls. Look for Cold Fyyre's ice cream made with fruit from the islands, Sky Kombucha's drinks with Hawaiian produce, and North Shore Cattle Company's sausages and burgers.
*609 Kailua Road*
*hfbf.org*

**①**
KCC Farmers' Market,
Diamond Head
*Start-up business*

This market, held on Saturday mornings from 07.30 in the Kapi'olani Community College car park, is a good spot for breakfast. There are more than 70 vendors selling flowers and fresh produce, all-natural ice lollies, Ka'u coffee, burgers, taro chips, farmed abalone and macadamia nuts.

KCC is also a springboard for entrepreneurs: The Pig & the Lady (*see page 32*) got its start here and its booth, featuring *banh mi* sandwiches and noodle soups, has the longest queues. On Tuesdays, there's a small evening market from 16.00.
*4303 Diamond Head Road*
*hfbf.org*

### Fish auction

Hours before sunrise the Honolulu Fish Auction on Pier 38 is a hive of activity. Operated by the non-profit Hawaii Seafood Council, the auction is one of the biggest in the US and the only one that has fresh tuna. Bigeye and yellowfin tuna, marlin, swordfish, moonfish and more are all line-caught; Hawaii's authorities prohibit trawl and seine nets. Reservation-only tours on Saturdays start at 06.00.
*hawaii-seafood.org*

③
Honolulu Farmers' Market,
Ala Moana
*Fresh pickings*

Don't miss New Brug Bakery's stall of freshly baked treats and Hanalei Taro's *poi* and hummus. You'll also find pizza made with Shinsato pork from Bonfire Pizza's Steven Wilson and lots of vegetables. It's open Wednesdays from 16.00 to 19.00 near the Neal S Blaisdell Center.
*777 Ward Avenue*
*hfbf.org*

④
Kaka'ako Farmers' Market, Kaka'ako
*Taste maker*

This event takes place on Saturdays from 08.00 to 12.00 in the Ward Warehouse parking lot. We recommend Daylight Mind Coffee Company (which sells Kona coffee) and North Shore's Hawaiian Fresh Farms, a honey and goat-cheese maker serving breakfast plates of buttermilk pancakes and *loco moco*.
*1240 Ala Moana Boulevard*
*farmloversmarkets.com*

## Desserts
Sweet spots

①
Leonard's Bakery, Kapahulu
*Go with the dough*

*Malasadas* – puffy, sugar-dusted deep-fried dough – arrived in Hawaii with Portuguese plantation workers in the late 19th century. But Leonard Rego, who started Leonard's Bakery in 1952, is widely credited with getting the Hawaiian masses addicted to the Portuguese doughnut.

The bakery no longer has a monopoly on *malasadas* but its shop on Kapahulu Avenue and Malasadamobile truck are still the best place to get this made-to-order treat. There is also a Japanese branch in Yokohama.
*933 Kapahulu Avenue*
*+ 1 808 737 5591*
*leonardshawaii.com*

### Rich history

Hawaii is the only US state with commercial cacao farms so it's the ideal base for bean-to-bar chocolate makers Madre Chocolate and Lonohana Chocolate. Their Hawaiian-grown cacao makes for a bright, fruity chocolate.
*madrechocolate.com;*
*lonohana.com*

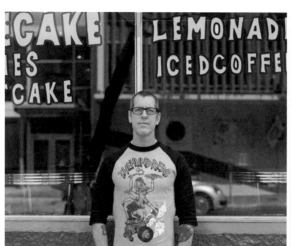

② 
Otto Cake, Kaimuki
*Delicious DIY*

Otto Cake began as a belated mother's day gift three decades ago – and owner Scott "Otto" McDonough (*pictured*) still makes his silky smooth cheesecakes as he did then, mixing every batch by hand and baking the cakes in standard kitchen ovens.

The interior is a funky blend of DIY and primary colours, a reflection of Otto's punk-rock roots (he is in the band The 86 List). Flavours change daily and according to seasonal availability but don't overlook the plain cheesecake. Cash only.
*1127 12th Avenue*
*+ 1 808 834 6886*
*ottocake.com*

③
Lemona Hawaii, Waikiki
*Big chill*

Located on the bottom floor of a two-storey residential complex, this shave-ice shop is identifiable by the writing on the windows. The shortlist of flavours is determined by what's in season so expect anything from mango to pomegranate. Always on the menu: Meyer lemon from Hawaii Island, pineapple from O'ahu and Kona coffee and matcha (made with ceremonial green tea).

The trifecta is matcha topped with azuki beans and condensed milk, which adds a creamy element to the finely shaved ice.
*421 Lewers Street*
*+ 1 808 922 9590*
*lemona-hi.com*

④
Kamehameha Bakery, Kalihi
*Sugar rush*

This bakery opens very early – at 02.00 – so expect to get your dessert for breakfast. Top of the list are the delightfully decadent glazed taro and strawberry *malasadas* (*see page 39*). They often sell out before noon.
*1284 Kalani Street*
*+ 1 808 845 5831*

⑤
Via Gelato, Kaimuki
*Cold comfort*

Melissa Bow started Via Gelato
out of a truck and quickly built
the momentum to debut this
charming neighbourhood shop
in Kaimuki, where the lights stay
on late and there is nearly always
a long queue.

Bow sources many of the
ingredients for her sorbetto and
gelato locally and Hawaiian culture
is reflected in flavours such as *ube*
(sweet potato) and *haupia* (coconut
milk dessert). Those with more
mainland tastes can also delight in
such offerings as Fierce Chocolate
and salted caramel with fudge.
*1142 12th Avenue*
*+1 808 732 2800*
*viagelato.com*

**Coffee shops**
Perfect brews

*Ready to go*
Fresh coffee
is the order of
the day here

①
Aloha Coffee Lab's The Curb
at Pan Am, Ala Moana
*Bean idols*

It's not easy to find espresso made
with Hawaii-grown beans, which
is why Tokunori Kuwahara's kiosk
deserves mention; he opts for
beans grown and roasted by farms
in Kona and Ka'u. A stickler for
freshness, he also uses all beans
within two weeks of roasting.
*1600 Kapiolani Boulevard*
*alohacoffeelab.com*

② 
Morning Glass Coffee + Café, Manoa
*Rise and shine*

Weekend brunch is a good excuse to drive out to Morning Glass Coffee + Café in Manoa Valley. Chicago native and former Starbucks executive Eric Rose and his staff make biscuits and gravy, savoury pancakes with macaroni and cheese, and omelettes of applewood smoked bacon or local Ali'i mushrooms.

The beans for drip coffee and espresso drinks come from Stumptown Coffee Roasters in Portland and Four Barrel Coffee in San Francisco, and there's usually a Hawaii-grown coffee that Rose roasts himself on the premises in small batches every few days. He makes a point of using produce grown on the islands for breakfast and lunch, with beef from Kulana Foods, pork from Shinsato Farms and freshly laid eggs from Ka Lei Eggs.

*2955 East Manoa Road*
*+ 1 808 673 0065*
*morningglasscoffee.com*

**Three takeaway coffee shops**

**01 ARS Café, Diamond Head**
3116 Monsarrat Avenue
*ars-cafe.com*

**02 The Curb, Kaimuki**
3538 Waialae Avenue
*thecurbco.com*

**03 Coffee Gallery, Hale'iwa**
66-250 Kamehameha Highway
*roastmaster.com*

**③**
Brue Bar, Downtown
*Caffeine highs*

Brue Bar has its roots in printing shop Honblue, where it was introduced in 2013 to give walk-in customers a place to wait or hold meetings. Now its three Honolulu shops – in which baristas make espressos on Slayer machines – are havens for coffee lovers.

Brue sources its beans from Hawaiian roaster Kona Coffee Purveyors and California-based Verve Coffee Roasters; its teas are from TeaSource in Minnesota while the desserts are made by O'ahu bakeries including Agnes Bake Shop in Kailua.
*119 Merchant Street*
*+ 1 808 441 4470*
*bruebar.com*

---

**Bars**
**Counter culture**

**①**
The Tchin Tchin! Bar, Chinatown
*Vermouth with a view*

This surprisingly spacious wine bar from the owners of neighbouring restaurants Livestock Tavern (*see page 31*) and Lucky Belly (*see page 32*) is located up a flight of stairs off Chinatown's Hotel Street. Its extensive drinks menu was the first in town to dedicate a full page to the syrupy sweetness that is vermouth.

Sip it chilled while sampling small plates such as *boquerones* (white anchovies) and oxtail rillettes at one of the enormous half-circle booths along the front windows. Or you can dine on the patio, which offers a rooftop view and sprawling couches.
*39 Hotel Street*
*+ 1 808 528 1888*
*thetchintchinbar.com*

---

**②**
Bar Leather Apron, Downtown
*Elite squad*

Tom Park and Justin Park (*both pictured, Tom on left*) have recreated the service and cocktails they enjoyed on trips to Japan with this intimate space. The best seats are at the bar facing the bartenders, led by Justin; this elite section has a drinks menu all of its own. Reservations are vital.
*Suite 127A, 745 Fort Street*
*+ 1 808 524 0808*
*barleatherapron.com*

---

**Halekulani hotel bars**

This five-star hotel on Waikiki Beach has three of the best bars in the city.

**01**  House Without a Key: Immortalised in the 1925 Charlie Chan novel of the same name, this breezy bar and restaurant is open from morning till night but its fame resides in its mai tais and the sunset show of music and dancing.

**02**  Lewers Lounge: With its wood panelling, cushioned banquettes and first-rate jazz pianist, Lewers Lounge is a sumptuous spot. Celebrated bartender Colin Field, of the Ritz in Paris, introduced a few signature originals such as the ginger lychee caipirissima.

**03**  L'Aperitif: The setting – a beachside villa designed for the hotel in 1932 – is utterly beguiling and the drinks are even better. Head bartender Henry Kawaiaea is a 30-year veteran; try one of his smoke-infused Red Nichols Manhattans.
*halekulani.com*

③
La Mariana Sailing Club, Kalihi
*Gaudy glory*

At one time there were numerous tiki bars around Honolulu revelling in the faux-Polynesian style that came straight from Hollywood. Today the only original one left is La Mariana, which opened in 1957. The throwback interior features grass-clad ceilings, a gaudy ornamental waterfall and cosy booths in which to sample a menu of American fare.

As other tiki joints have closed, La Mariana has become a repository for their memorabilia, such as the carved tikis from Kon Tiki at the Sheraton and koa-wood tables from the legendary Don the Beachcomber bar.
*50 Sand Island Access Road*
*+1 808 848 2800*
*lamarianasailingclub.com*

**Still standing**
—
La Mariana is one of the last original tiki bars

## Purveyors and producers
### Buy your own

HASR Wine Company, Chinatown
*Sophisticated bottles*

This wine shop, owned by Mike and Terry Kakazu, faces the same courtyard as HASR Bistro. Its speciality is top-end Californian wine but you can find bottles from around the world too. Uncork your favourite with a meal from the bistro or try the wine tasting every Tuesday and Friday.
*31 North Pauahi Street*
*+1 808 535 9463*
*hasrwineco.com*

②
The Sake Shop, Ala Moana
*Rare finds*

Its consumption is on the rise in the US, yet until Nadine and Malcolm Leong opened this shop in 2010, Hawaii had no retailers of premium saké. The selection runs the gamut from inexpensive bottles to rare finds, including undiluted *genshu* of the calibre prized by connoisseurs.
*1461 South King Street*
*+1 808 947 7253*
*sakeshophawaii.com*

③
Village Bottle Shop & Tasting Room, Kaka'ako
*All that jazz*

Don't call it a bar. What co-founders Tim Golden and Daryn Ogino had in mind for Village Bottle Shop & Tasting Room in Kaka'ako is closer to a liquor shop that specialises in craft beers but also has a selection of beers and wines on tap.

Golden, the founder of the Beer in Hawaii blog, and Ogino, a partner at Pint + Jigger bar, opened their shop in mid-2016 because they wanted to overturn conventional perceptions about beer. Golden is also a certified cicerone (beer expert) and can tell you what types of food go well with specific brews.
*333 Keawe Street*
*villagebeerhawaii.com*

④
Manulele Distillers, Kunia Camp
*A rum do*

Cultivation of Hawaii's sugar cane dates back to the earliest settlers centuries ago but few people knew much about its heirloom varieties until Robert Dawson started making rum in 2014. Dawson co-founded Manulele Distillers, turning out small batches of single-variety Ko Hana agricole rum from cane grown on his partner Jason Brand's farm in Kunia.

Manulele uses freshly pressed juice, a yeast strain isolated from Hawaii-grown cacao plants and ancient cane varieties to make the clear rum. The distillery is open for tours and tastings.
*92-1770 Kunia Road*
*+1 808 649 0830*
*kohanarum.com*

⑤
Honolulu Beerworks, Kaka'ako
*Brew Hawaii*

At this warehouse-like space, brewer Geoff Seideman keeps the taps flowing with a rotating line-up of at least 10 beers. His potent Animal Farmhouse Ale, Barrel Rye'd and Citrus Saison are winners. The brewery has stepped up production since opening in 2014.
*328 Cooke Street*
*+1 808 589 2337*
*honolulubeerworks.com*

⑥
Hawaiian Shochu Company, Hale'iwa
*That's the spirit*

Ken and Yumiko Hirata make 6,000 bottles of sweet potato *shochu* (a distilled liquor) each year. The vegetables are abundant in Honolulu and the Hiratas get theirs locally. Make a booking to buy a bottle; they sell out quickly.
*66-542 Haleiwa Road, entrance on Paalaa Road*
*kaloimo.exblog.jp*

# Retail
## —— The goods

Tourist-jammed Waikiki is the obvious place to stock up on clothes, souvenirs and knick-knacks. But shopping here is rarely rewarding and if you don't venture farther afield you will miss out. We have searched the city for surfboards shaped by hand, Panama and lauhala hats, vintage aloha shirts, letterpress stationery, handmade ceramics and all manner of distinctive off-the-wall goods.

You will find these items in small shops scattered around Honolulu; in Chinatown, McCully-Mo'ili'ili and Diamond Head and other, less familiar neighbourhoods. And a visit to these stores will bring you face to face with the ever-expanding group of proprietors who are exploring new ideas and championing the work of artists, craftspeople, designers and lesser-known brands to sell products that you won't find anywhere else.

**Mixed bag**
Top shops

① 
Mono, McCully-Mo'ili'ili
*Colourful curios*

*Mono* is Japanese for "things", although that doesn't quite cover the huge array of well-made lifestyle and office goods that owners Dean and Cassy Song sell: Ogami notebooks from Italy, Düller stationery from Japan, Unit Portables pouches from Sweden, Porter bags from Japan and Hawaiian artwork and books.

The idea of opening a shop originated on a honeymoon trip to Japan where the couple fell in love with products with understated, functional design. Such finds are among the regularly updated selection at their minimalist space.
*2013 South King Street*
*+1 808 955 1595*
*monohawaii.com*

*Soft landings are crucial when you're an owl*

**②**

Mori by Art + Flea, Kaka'ako
*Market trading*

Aly Ishikuni-Sasaki and Nicole Franco started Art + Flea in 2010 as an occasional market where Honolulu's independent makers could show and sell their work. Four years on Ishikuni-Sasaki (*pictured, right*) opened her Mori by Art + Flea shop to sell stationery, clothing, crafts, magazines and grooming products.

As well as being the vocalist for pop-rock band Alt/Air, Ishikuni-Sasaki also finds time to organise Art + Flea's monthly events and holds weekly workshops, product launches and music performances in the shop.
*Ward Warehouse, 1050 Ala Moana Boulevard,
+1 808 593 8958
artandflea.com*

**Flea spirits**
—
The monthly market has more than 60 sellers

**Family institution**

Sidney and Minnie Kosasa opened the first ABC Store in Waikiki in 1964, selling health and beauty products. Today it's a Honolulu-based convenience-store chain of more than 70 shops run by their son Paul. You will find everything to fulfil a traveller's needs, from suntan lotion, towels, clothes and souvenirs to bento meals, wine, Hawaiian coffee beans and made-to-order sandwiches. The staff all wear aloha shirts and perma-smiles.
*abcstores.com*

**4**

South Shore Paperie, Kaimuki
*Stationery of note*

There are two antique letterpress machines in the back of South Shore Paperie. Co-owner Ian Nomura uses them to print designs by his wife, Stacey, on recycled paper for Bradley & Lily Fine Stationery, the brand the couple named after their two children. The shop is a letter-writer's dream; cards line the walls and spill over onto tables, including stacks of notes and stationery by other printers in Hawaii. Write home on a set of cards stamped with a golden "aloha", pick up a hula-style birthday card or jot your thoughts in a mini notebook with a shave-ice-cone print.
*1016 Kapahulu Avenue*
*+ 1 808 744 8746*
*southshorepaperie.com*

*Now this is the kind of place I can fly a flag for*

**3**

Hound & Quail, Chinatown
*Quirky finds*

German-made wooden toy villages, handcrafted pewter flasks from the UK, a stuffed ostrich head, gumball machines and aged US flags are among the antiques and oddities that Mark Pei and Travis Flazer have rescued from estate sales and flea markets in Hawaii and beyond. There's no clutter: everything is hung on the walls or neatly arranged in cases resembling a natural history museum. The pair opened the shop in 2007 and upgraded to the current space seven years later. They also host art shows, wine tastings and food events in the basement.
*920 Maunakea Street*
*+ 1 808 779 8436*
*houndandquail.com*

⑤
Kamaka Hawaii, Kaka'ako
*First family of ukuleles*

Hawaii's oldest ukulele manufacturer was founded by Sam Kamaka in 1916 and is now owned by his sons and managed by his grandsons (*see page 71*). The company is known for its bulbous four-string pineapple-shaped ukulele (patented in 1928). Its workshop in Honolulu produces the four basic types – soprano, tenor, concert and baritone – for top musicians including Jake Shimabukuro, Eddie Kamae and Herb Ohta. The workshop opens for morning tours that are occasionally led by nonagenarian Fred Kamaka (*pictured, top right*), one of Sam's sons.
*550 South Street*
*+1 808 531 3165*
*kamakahawaii.com*

Note perfect
—
Three generations have run the workshop

Sound bite

The word "ukulele" means "jumping flea" in Hawaiian. Its design was inspired by the *braguinha*, a small string instrument that was brought to the islands by Portuguese immigrants in the 19th century.

Ⓖ
Island Paddler, Kapahulu
*Love boat*

Hawaii's first outrigger canoe race took place in 1917 but for thousands of years before that these slender boats with a beam on one side were used on the open seas. Today outrigger canoeing – or "paddling" as it's known in Hawaii – is the state's official team sport, with races for one to six-person canoes open to a world-class field. Island Paddler, opened in 1998 by Ronald Cotteen, Eric Phillips and Leigh Tonai, stocks the sport's essentials: gloves, shorts, shirts and more than 300 paddles made from wood (mahogany, balsa, redwood) and graphite.
*716 Kapahulu Avenue*
*+1 808 737 4854*
*islandpaddlerhawaii.com*

### The big paddle

The Moloka'i Hoe, a 65km race in October between the Hawaiian islands of Moloka'i and O'ahu, is the premier annual outrigger canoe race and one of the state's biggest events. The contest started in 1952 with just three canoes but now attracts in excess of 1,000 paddlers.

⑦
Aloha Stadium Swap Meet, Aiea
*Treasure hunt*

This garage sale, craft fair and farmers' market is where secondhand connoisseurs hunt for collectibles. Staged in the stadium car park on Wednesdays and weekends, the meet began in 1979 and now has more than 400 vendors who sell antiques, jewellery, food and clothing.
*99-500 Salt Lake Boulevard*
*+1 808 486 6704*
*alohastadiumswapmeet.net*

**Take your pick**
The shop stocks more than 15,000 aloha shirts

⑩
Tin Can Mailman, Chinatown
*Retro collectibles*

Owner Christopher Oswalt's shop is a trove of Hawaiian collectibles. Packing the shelves and racks are linen postcards, fruit labels, vintage aloha shirts, tiki mugs and hula-girl nodding dolls. The collection, which has grown since Oswalt (*pictured*) took over in 2003, draws on souvenirs dating from Hawaii's mid-century tourism boom and includes hard-to-find items, including many Hawaii-themed books: telephone directories, novels, out-of-print travelogues and coffee-table tomes. You're sure to unearth something unique to take home.
*1026 Nuuanu Avenue*
*+1 808 524 3009*
*tincanmailman.net*

⑨
Pauahi Leis & Flowers, Chinatown
*Flower power*

Lei are a well-known tradition in Hawaii, given on special occasions such as birthdays or anniversaries. At this small decades-old shop you can find ladies making garlands at a table strewn with orchid, tuberose and plumeria blossoms. Watch them string one with fresh blooms or weave intricate Micronesian ginger lei.
*1145 Maunakea Street*
*+1 808 521 6156*

❽
Bailey's Antiques and Aloha Shirts, Kapahulu
*Get shirty*

For anyone even remotely interested in the state's famed attire, David Bailey's shop is the holy grail. He has amassed a collection of more than 15,000 aloha shirts, some dating back to the 1930s, in every hue and pattern imaginable. These have been classified into four categories – used, new, vintage and speciality – and take up almost all of the wall space of this hard-to-miss pink building. Shirt aficionados go out of their way to unearth rare finds here; there's also a colourful selection of kitsch ephemera to peruse.
*517 Kapahulu Avenue*
*+1 808 734 7628*
*alohashirts.com*

⑪
The Bungalow Hawaii, Chinatown
*Heirs and graces*

This whimsical florist and interior-design studio was opened in November 2015 by Nancy Parnell and her daughter Lauren Paultz (*pictured*). Directly across the street from the wonderful Hound & Quail (*see page 48*), The Bungalow Hawaii stocks a thoughtful and eclectic collection of vintage trinkets, from lovely old paintings of Hawaiian shorelines to bronze pineapple-shaped paperweights and reclaimed porcelain from the Royal New Zealand Navy.
*925 Maunakea Street*
*+1 808 799 3238*
*bungalowhawaii.com*

⑫
Fishcake, Kaka'ako
*Design-minded homeware*

Maura Fujihara's shop – named after the pink-and-white slices of processed fish in *saimin* noodles – specialises in art, furniture, tableware and homeware accessories made by Hawaiian entrepreneurs and artists. You'll find woven baskets by Amelia Samari, celadon ceramic plates by Steve Martin and *furoshiki* wrapping cloth by Donna Miyashiro.

Fujihara also has a design firm that creates interiors for bars and restaurants. You don't need to go far to see an example: the Morning Glass Coffee + Pastry Bar is inside the shop. We recommend the coffee too.
*307c Kamani Street*
*+1 808 593 1231*
*fishcake.us*

⑬
Hungry Ear Records,
McCully-Mo'ili'ili
*Top of the shops*

With 50,000 new and secondhand records, Honolulu's oldest vinyl shop has plenty to satisfy fans of rock, punk, folk, jazz and alternative music. What puts it in a class of its own is the Hawaiian section: the early recordings of 1950s slack-key guitarist Gabby Pahinui; the albums of 1970s rock, jazz, funk and disco-influenced groups such as Cecilio & Kapono and the Mackey Feary Band; and today's homegrown crooners and reggae artists.

Amateur music historians and Hungry Ear owners Ward (*pictured*) and Mary Yamashita moved the shop to its present location in 2014 from Kailua, where it started under different ownership in 1980. Ask them to play any record in the store before you make a purchase. You can also pick up turntables, needles and more.
*2615 South King Street*
*+1 808 262 2175*
*hungryear.com*

Crate diggers
—
Hungry Ear Records caters to all tastes

**⑭**
Treehouse, Kaka'ako
*Focus on film*

*Treehouse is the place for a shutterdog such as myself*

When Bobby Asato opened Treehouse, tucked away on the second floor of a nondescript building, the focus was firmly on arts and crafts for kids. A few years later his shop is the place to go for expertise on all things photography-related. Here you'll find film (Kodak, Impossible, Ilford, you name it) and analogue cameras ranging from used Contax point-and-shoots to new Instax instant film cameras. Come here to pick up a roll of black-and-white film, flip through design books or get your film developed. And the children's craft kits are still available.
*233/250 Ward Avenue*
*+ 1 808 597 8733*
*treehouse-shop.com*

⑮
## Hakubundo, Kaka'ako
*Print Japan*

Hakubundo was founded in 1910 to sell Japanese products to Hawaii. The brand now has two shops in Kaka'ako. At the older Ward Warehouse location (*pictured, top*), J-pop fills the air while San-X plushies, anime and accessories pack the shelves. The Ward Centre branch (*pictured, bottom*) stocks stationery such as erasable pens, animal clips and patterned tapes, as well as magazines and books.
*Ward Warehouse:*
*1050 Ala Moana Boulevard*
*+1 808 591 2134*
*Ward Centre:*
*1200 Ala Moana Boulevard*
*+1 808 947 5503*
*hakubundo.com*

⑯
Honolulu Museum of Art Shop, Makiki
*Coffee-table fodder*

This museum's collection is broad-ranging and so are its bookshelves: modernist architect Vladimir Ossipoff, traditional featherwork and Hawaiian quilts are all represented here, along with stationery, prints and postcards.
*900 South Beretania Street*
*+1 808 532 8703*
*shop.honolulumuseum.org*

⑰
## Greenroom Hawaii, Waikiki
*Living colour*

Naoki Kamayachi's first Greenroom shop, opened in Japan in 2005, grew out of the success of his Greenroom Festival in Yokohama that showcases surfing and beach-related music, art and film. Kamayachi teamed up with Jun Yoshimura, owner of Good Art Animation, to open Greenroom in Waikiki in 2010. It's predominantly an outlet for surf-inspired oil paintings and prints by

artists such as Tyler Warren, Yusuke Hanai and Susan Wickstrand but it also sells books and clothes.
*2255 Kalakaua Avenue (inside Sheraton Waikiki)*
*+1 808 931 8908*
*greenroomhawaii.com*

⑱
## Idea's Music and Books, Kaka'ako
*Books of knowledge*

This vast shop is a warehouse of wonders in which it's easy to lose yourself for hours. The aisles are stacked with thousands of used and new records next to rare books, vintage comics and secondhand titles. Owner Norm Winter has been buying records for 40 years and is an authority on Hawaiian music; the collection of old records here is a revelation. "We're always hoping to find something awesome," says Shirley Neely, the shop's manager and book-buyer. "And pretty often, we do."
*670 Auahi Street*
*+1 808 545 5002*
*ideasmusicandbooks.com*

**Clothing**
Island fashion

High stepping
—
Leather Soul stocks designer footwear

**1**

Leather Soul, Downtown
*If the shoe fits*

It can't be easy selling high-class shoe brands Alden, JW Weston and John Lobb in the tropics. But regulars at Leather Soul's shops (there is a second in Waikiki) are thankful for Tom Park's dedication to raising Hawaii's sartorial standards.

Park's Alden line-up includes some exclusive models and he also stocks trainers, Oxford shirts from US brand Individualized Shirts and aloha shirts produced in Hawaii through a collaboration with Reyn Spooner. The shop, overseen by manager Justin Cariaga (*pictured*), also offers a shoe-shine service.
*119 Merchant Street*
*+1 808 523 7700*
*leathersoul.com*

I need one for each day of the week

**②**

James After Beach Club,
Diamond Head
*Japanese style*

The first US shop for Kamakura-
based James & Co designer
Masayoshi Shioya sells wardrobe
basics with universal appeal: unisex
chambray, plaid and Oxford shirts,
linen shorts and ultra-soft T-shirts,
all made in Japan. You will also find
handmade surfboards whose colour
evokes the sunburnt foam used by
1960s waveriders – a collaboration
between Shioya and Honolulu-
based custom boardmaker
Todd Pinder (*see page 59*). The
music comes from manager Junji
Hashimoto's vinyl collection.
*3045 Monsarrat Avenue*
*+ 1 808 737 8982*
*james-hawaii.com*

### Weaving a story
───

As many as 30 pandanus
leaves go into every lauhala hat.
Techniques have traditionally
been closely guarded family
secrets but master weaver
Gladys Kukana Grace, who
died in 2013, passed on her
knowledge through lessons and
a club she co-founded in 1997.

## Menswear

**01** Salvage Public: Menswear
brand Salvage Public was
founded in 2013 by
Oʻahu-born brothers
Joseph and Noah Serrao
and their friend Napali
Souza. Their handsome
boardshorts, T-shirts,
hats, sweatshirts and
button-down shirts are
manufactured in the US.
*salvagepublic.com*

**02** Quality Peoples: Former
Diesel creative supervisor
John Esguerra, now based
on the North Shore, and
Ed Fladung, who lives in
Mexico, started this brand
in 2010, building it around
casual menswear with
understated design.
*qualitypeoples.com*

**03** Eroix: Kailua-based
husband-and-wife team
Parker and Jenn Ellenburg
think of their product as
"underneathwear": cotton
boxer shorts that don't
bunch up and can
be worn to the beach
without anyone knowing
you've left the house in
your underpants.
*eroix.com*

**04** Aloha Beach Club and
Shoots: Brothers Kahana
and Kamohai Kalama and
co-founder Billy Wickens
have two brands: Shoots,
which produces chairs,
rugs and towels; and
Aloha Beach Club, which
specialises in Oxford shirts,
blazers, beachwear and
aloha shirts.
*alohabeachclub.com*

**05** M.Nii: This brand began
as a tailoring shop making
shorts for surfers from the
1940s to the 1960s. It was
revived as a menswear line
by California-based
designer John Moore in
2011 but it still has its roots
in mid-century Hawaiian
beach culture.
*mnii.com*

③
We Are Iconic, Ala Moana
*Feminine charm*

This bright, spacious boutique, located across the street from the busy Ala Moana Center mall, is a breath of fresh air. Racks are filled with owner Shie Clark's favourite finds from womenswear brands such as Ace & Jig, Wilt and No 6; tables are sparsely topped with Le Feu de l'Eau candles and Clare V clutches.

Clark ventured into retail with an online boutique 10 years ago before opening this shop in 2013. Her collection of contemporary urban clothing is a standout among Honolulu's womenswear shops.
*1236 Waimanu Street*
*+1 808 462 4575*
*shopweareiconic.com*

④
Newt at The Royal, Waikiki
*Hats off*

The aloha spirit is alive and well at this compact shop in The Royal Hawaiian hotel. Newt sells some of the finest Panama hats on the market. Lee Lockhart makes the trip to Montecristi in Ecuador (home of the best Panamas) to handpick the hats. He sends them to his expert hatter in Chicago where they are completed with a black grosgrain ribbon and Roan sweatband leather. Also on sale are Newt's own cotton aloha shirts with retro prints from the 1940s and 1950s, finished with bamboo, coconut or mother-of-pearl buttons.
*2259 Kalakaua Avenue*
*+1 808 923 4332*
*newtattheroyal.com*

### Two more shirt shops

Aloha shirts are ubiquitous in Hawaii and the two big brands for this iconic item are Tori Richard and Reyn Spooner. Here are two more places where you can find new threads.

**01**  Rix Island Wear, Kaka'ako
Specialises in bold and tribal designs on cotton shirts that are sewn in Hawaii.
*rixislandwear.com*

**02**  Kahala Sportswear, Ala Moana
Classic prints of Hawaiian fauna and flora, from the early Waikiki beachboy days, by a brand that was founded in 1936.
*kahala.com*

## Surfboards and beachwear
### New wave

### ① Clips, Ala Moana
*Surf specialist*

Makoto Kambara (*pictured*) doesn't cater to the mainstream at the small surf shop he took over and reopened in 2014. He sells wooden surfboards made by Firewire from sustainably grown Paulownia trees and environmentally friendly resin, alongside pro-calibre boards by Nat Woolley of Woolley Brothers and shaper Wade Tokoro. Kambara's racks also feature clothing by Hawaiian brands Salvage Public, Plate Lunch and Quality Peoples, and he also stocks plenty of swimsuits, womenswear and beach essentials.
*822 Kaheka Street*
*+1 808 941 6777*
*clipshawaii.com*

### ② Aloha Boardshop, McCully-Moʻiliʻili
*Under the sun*

Owner Karim Hammani has an extensive line-up of new and used surfboards, skateboards and accessories and friendly, helpful staff. Billed as a "one-stop surf and skate shop", the South King Street outpost is conveniently located for the South Shore's fine beaches.
*2658 South King Street*
*+1 808 955 6030*
*alohaboardshop.com*

### ③ Island Slipper, Ala Moana
*Firm footing*

Hawaii's oldest footwear brand is also the only one with its factory on the islands. The company was started by Takizo and Misao Motonaga in the 1940s and passed on to John and Daisy Carpenter in 1984. Today it manufactures more than 80 kinds of sandals.
*1450 Ala Moana Boulevard*
*+1 808 947 1222*
*islandslipper.com*

④
### T&C Surf Design, Ala Moana
*Off the shelf*

Craig Sugihara opened Town & Country Surf in Pearl City in 1971, selling his handcrafted surfboards. Today the T&C Surf brand is a widely recognised leader in custom-made and off-the-shelf boards (from its factory in Wahiawa, O'ahu), fins and clothing.
*1450 Ala Moana Boulevard*
*+1 808 973 5199*
*tcsurf.com*

⑤
### Local Motion, citywide
*Beach pickings*

Local Motion got its start in 1977 as a surfboard brand and now has nine shops in Hawaii, five of them on O'ahu. Its boards are made by Hawaii's elite shapers – Wade Tokoro, Carl Schaper and Ricky Carroll – for pro surfers but the company sells plenty of essentials for the surfing hobbyist too.
*+1 808 979 7873*
*localmotionhawaii.com*

⑥
### Downing Hawaii, Kaimuki
*Generation game*

Surfing is a Downing family tradition. George Downing, one of Hawaii's big-wave surfing pioneers, opened this shop in 1968 and it's now run by his children, Keone and Kaiulu. They can recommend a board or tell you about the history of surfing and outrigger canoe racing in Hawaii.
*3021 Waialae Avenue*
*+1 808 737 9696*
*downingsurf.com*

### Custom surfboards

Todd Pinder is an old-fashioned surfboard builder who does every step – shaping, glassing, painting and sanding – by hand in his workshop. There's a four-month wait for the custom creations but James After Beach Club (*see page 56*) stocks a selection of his manila-hued 1960s-style longboards.
*surfboardsbytoddpinder.com*

# Things we'd buy
## —— Island treasures

Nothing says Hawaiian holiday like an aloha shirt, a palm-tree-print pouch or a pair of surfing shorts. For this product round-up we scoured O'ahu and favoured items sewn, grown, brewed, shaped, recorded and woven on the islands; the resulting mix includes hand-thrown ceramics, Hawaiian tunes on vinyl, bright aloha shirts and coffee beans. We guarantee you'll find a meaningful memento among their number.

**01** Pillow from Hawaiian Quilt Collection at The Royal Hawaiian *+1 808 922 2462*
**02** Women's sandals from Island Slipper *islandslipper.com*
**03** Hat by Evva Lim of Friends of Ulana Me Ka Lokomaika'i from Shop Pacifica *bishopmuseum.org*
**04** Beans by Aloha Coffee Lab *alohacoffeelab.com*
**05** Agricole rum by Manulele Distillers *kohanarum.com*
**06** *Party Hulas* vinyl from Idea's Music and Books *ideasmusicandbooks.com*
**07** Malie Organics body wash from Spa Halekulani *halekulani.com*
**08** Room spray from Paiko *paikohawaii.com*
**09** Hand-poured soy candles from Mono *monohawaii.com*
**10** *Hawaiian Slack Key Guitar* CD from Dancing Cat Records *dancingcat.com*
**11** Namihana shochu from Hawaiian Shochu Company *kaloimo.exblog.jp*
**12** Royal Mills Hawaiian Kona coffee from ABC Stores *abcstores.com*
**13** *Instant Hawaiian* by Chris Christensen from Bernice Pauahi Bishop Museum shop *bishopmuseum.org*
**14** *The Hawaiian Survival Handbook* by Brother Noland from Paiko *paikohawaii.com*
**15** Tutu Nene goose from Hawaiian Mission Houses Gift Shop *missionhouses.org*
**16** Bottle opener by Mau-Haus *mau-house.com*
**17** Manoa Lump charcoal soap from Green Mountain *greenmountainhawaii.com*
**18** Reyn Spooner × Leather Soul aloha shirt from Leather Soul *leathersoul.com*
**19** Ukulele from Ukulele PuaPua *gcea.com*
**20** Aloha shirt from Tori Richard *toririchard.com*
**21** Shirt from Bailey's Antiques and Aloha Shirts *alohashirts.com*
**22** DaFin swimming fins by Zak Noyle *dafin.com*
**23** Sea + Current pouch from Roberta Oaks *robertaoaks.com*

**24** Samudra pouch from Aloha
Superette *alohasuperette.com*
**25** Steve Martin ceramics from
Fishcake *fishcake.us*
**26** Children's T-shirt by T&C
Surf Design *tcsurf.com*
**27** Quality Peoples T-shirt from
No 808 *number808.com*
**28** James & Co T-shirt from
James After Beach Club
*james-hawaii.com*

**29** Bradley & Lily Postcards
from South Shore Paperie
*southshorepaperie.com*
**30** Yusuke Hanai print
from Greenroom Hawaii
*greenroomhawaii.com*
**31** Nick Kuchar print
from Greenroom Hawaii
*greenroomhawaii.com*
**32** Eroix underwear from Oliver
*oliverhawaii.com*

**33** Board shorts by Aloha
Beach Club
*alohabeachclub.com*
**34** Shoots towel from Aloha
Beach Club
*alohabeachclub.com*

# 12 essays
—— Honolulu
throughout history

**1**
Tour de force
*A native's guide*
*by Tomos Lewis,*
*Monocle*

**2**
In plain sight
*Hawaiian sense of place*
*by Timothy A Schuler,*
*architecture writer*

**3**
Keep your shirt on
*Fashion favourite*
*by Dale Hope,*
*author*

**4**
A stroke of pluck
*Making music*
*by Frederick Kamaka Sr,*
*ukulele maker*

**5**
Attention Spam
*Slippery staple*
*by Martha Cheng,*
*food writer*

**6**
The King and I
*Hawaii's main man*
*by Jerry Hopkins,*
*writer*

**7**
Small gains
*State of the art*
*by Pegge Hopper,*
*painter and gallerist*

**8**
Making waves
*Surf's up*
*by Laura Blears,*
*former professional surfer*

**9**
Pulling the strings
*Guitar hero*
*by George Kahumoku Jr,*
*slack-key guitarist*

**10**
Gift of the gab
*Literary legacy*
*by Stephanie Han,*
*teacher and writer*

**11**
Song and dance
*All hail hula*
*by Skyler Kamaka,*
*hula dancer*

**12**
Hitting a home run
*A jogger's tour*
*by David Y Ige,*
*governor of Hawaii*

*These excellent essays have inspired me to write one myself!*

ESSAY OI

# Tour de force
## *A native's guide*

———

The pages of a native's guidebook provide a unique introduction to Honolulu. The question is, published 40 years ago, do they reveal more about how Hawaii has changed or what has remained remarkably the same?

*by Tomos Lewis,
Monocle*

"Aloha!" says the elderly woman at the end of the phone, her voice cheery and warm. "Welcome to Dial-A-Prayer. If you would like to hear an inspirational message, please hold the line. If you would like to leave a prayer request, please press pound at any time." I hold the line.

The woman explains in a gentle, buttery drawl that amid life's chaos the divine can still be found, even in a place as bustling and as boisterous as Honolulu. "Please, please remember," she says, "that God loves you very much." Good to know, I think to myself, having indulged rather whole-heartedly in the earthly delights of Hawaii's state-

capital – all in the name of work, of course.

"God bless," she says, as the automated message draws to a close and the beep of a voicemail rings in my ear. This is where I am meant to leave my prayer request. My mind goes blank. I hang up the phone. No salvation for me then.

I had found this telephone number printed in the directory pages of *A Native's Guide to Honolulu and the Island of Oʻahu*, a travel guide written by the eminent Hawaiian author and historian George S Kanahele (1930-2000), published in 1976.

Its neon-pink cover – printed with bright stylised flowers – had caught my eye while I was browsing the shelves of a secondhand bookshop in Honolulu's Chinatown. I began leafing through its yellowed pages.

"I thought it was about time for a native Hawaiian to write a modern guide about his own Hawaii," says Kanahele in his introduction to the book. He was a celebrated native Hawaiian historian and writer. An authority on Asia Pacific affairs, he became a prominent proponent for what he described as "Hawaiian values". The erosion of the indigenous cultures and languages on the islands spurred him to lead the campaign to stem the advancing tide of homogenisation.

As I thumbed the pages of the book, I wondered what Kanahele's "own Hawaii" might have been like. Would he recognise this tropical metropolis today, I thought, 40 years on from when he penned his native's guide to his home city?

So I set myself a task: to find out what had changed and what had remained wonderfully the same. And the Dial-A-Prayer telephone number – listed in the Help section below the numbers for babysitters, city hall and a dentist – seemed like the perfect place to start. And praise be, it still worked, offering automated salvation to those indulging in Honolulu's heady charms today as it did 40 years ago.

The Honolulu that Kanahele paints is a vibrant place. "It is a city of a thousand cities where men, ideas, customs, religions and aspirations have converged in what is truly surprising – the most isolated speck of land on the surface of the Earth."

It is a sentiment that still resonates today. Honolulu, a city of half a million people, is home to 34 foreign consulates representing countries from Morocco to Micronesia, Sri Lanka to Sweden. Add to that daily air connections by most major airlines, which brought a record eight million visitors to the islands in 2014, and Honolulu's "ethnic potpourri", as Kanahele puts it, is as colourful as it was 40 years ago.

Kanahele revels in the singularity of his home territory.

He explains that far from being stifled by their geographical solitude, these "mere dots on the map" have always considered themselves to be at the centre of life, rather than at its fringes. "Remote though they may be," he writes, "old Hawaiians did not think of Hawaii as being a point in 'nowhere'. On the contrary, Hawaii, they believed, was the 'navel of the universe', a central point from which they were free to move about the Pacific world."

That sense of discovery weaves its way through every page of Kanahele's guide. There is a genuine joy in his prose, a rare tone for a guidebook: from the beauty of the islands' flora and fauna to the simple poetry of Hawaii's native languages and the quiet work of the torchlight fishermen. The latter would wade out into the waters at dusk with a spear in one hand and a burning torch in the other, peppering the darkening sea with bright dots of light – an unusual sight today.

But some features of the Honolulu experience require something of a warning, according to Kanahele, who picks out the gems of this city "of contrasts and surprises". The star draw at Honolulu Zoo, he says, is a pig – this is still

*"Honolulu's 'ethnic potpourri', as Kanahele puts it, is as colourful as it was 40 years ago"*

**Past delights**
—
**01 Hula Bowl**
Hawaii's American football extravaganza ended in 2008.
**02 Torchlight fishermen**
Few fishermen now stalk the waters with burning torches.
**03 Naked waiting staff**
Your supper won't be brought to you in the buff anymore, unfortunately.

true today – and many of the city's restaurants boast "topless" or "naked" waiting staff. (Sadly this is one feature of Honolulu hospitality that has slipped into the history books; perhaps I was looking in the wrong places.)

As guidebooks go, Kanahele's certainly has something of an agenda. His aim was to scratch away at the rather 2D image of itself that Hawaii had become: a tourist trap that reinforced the preconceptions of hula girls, grass skirts and flowery rituals that many first-time visitors came armed with. It was an experience that left little room for the nuance and the poetry of this place Kanahele called home.

"Below-the-surface tensions do exist," writes Kanahele of the relationship between native Hawaiians and "newcomers" to the islands. Efforts to address those tensions – which have not been marked by the violence or mass upheaval seen in some minority-rights struggles elsewhere – have been made in the years since *A Native's Guide to*

*Honolulu and the Island of O'ahu* was published. The Hawaiian language was granted official status in 1978, making Hawaii the only state in the union with two official languages; in 2015, Pidgin became the state's third official tongue. The 1993 Apology Resolution, signed by president Bill Clinton, acknowledged the US's role in overthrowing Hawaii's monarchy and went some way – though not entirely – to quelling the debate.

The Honolulu that Kanahele sketches in his guide is a curiosity – and it remains so today. It is still something of a picture postcard of an island paradise, brought boisterously to life. There are joys to revel in and quiet tensions to address. But, as Kanahele writes, "Hawaii is surely a different kind of experience and this native's perspective should help you find something unique."

"Most of all," he adds, "it should help you discover something about yourself again." And that, from this first-time visitor's point of view, it certainly did. — (M)

ABOUT THE WRITER: Tomos Lewis is MONOCLE's bureau chief in Toronto. He spends his days trying to master the ukulele – bought in Honolulu – while wearing a vintage aloha shirt that he snapped up at Bailey's Antiques in Waikiki. *A Native's Guide to Honolulu and the Island of O'ahu* (1976) is currently out of print.

# In plain sight
## *Hawaiian sense of place*

———

The architecture in Honolulu can seem somewhat lacklustre. But take it in conjunction with the environment and you'll discover a respect for cultural history and a flair for contemporary design.

*by Timothy A Schuler, architecture writer*

It was early afternoon and the building stopped me dead. Hidden by a curve in the street, its steep copper roofs were such a departure from the rest of the city that in spite of their overt reference to native Hawaiian architecture they seemed somehow alien – made all the more foreign by the weird, retro-futurist towers just behind them.

I parked my bike and wandered through the unusual building. A giant oculus and a long wall of reflective glass, which multiplied the copper roofs, transformed what was a relatively small building into an immersive, otherworldly maze. The structure was so well integrated with the surrounding landscape that it became difficult to know whether I was indoors or out, upstairs or down.

Such experiences are rare in Honolulu, a city that is big and bland and largely uninteresting, architecturally. The city sprawls some 25 miles along O'ahu's south shore, its white tendrils snaking up into the mountains, claiming every square inch of buildable land it can.

Over the years, however, I've come to see the island's lack of jaw-dropping architecture as a sign of Hawaii's engagement with its built environment – and not the other way around. Hawaiians would never stand for a Frank Gehry building; what works in other places won't work here.

About a decade after the building boom that followed statehood in 1959, the islands experienced a resurgence in native Hawaiian cultural practices: hula was revived as a serious dance form; Hawaiian was re-established as an official language and began to be taught in schools; and farmers began growing taro in traditional *lo'i kalo* (taro patches).

This cultural renaissance raised a question for architects: what should contemporary Hawaiian architecture look like? This was the context for the Kamakakuokalani Center for Hawaiian Studies, the building that would stop me in my tracks decades later. For years, many Hawaiians had spent time and money fighting developers, staving off the wholesale conversion of the island's coastline into a ring of resorts and its agricultural lands into sprawling suburbs. What would it look like to take that respect for the land and channel it into a building?

The need for a permanent home for the university's new Hawaiian studies programme provided the perfect opportunity to find out. The resulting structure, designed by Dwight Kauahikaua and Daniel Chun, recalls the *hale* (traditional house) of pre-contact Hawaii, its roofs and central courtyard giving occupants the feeling that the building is really

*"I've come to see the island's lack of jaw-dropping architecture as a sign of Hawaii's engagement with its built environment"*

several smaller buildings, like an early Hawaiian village. Copper stands in for thatch and seams in the copper-clad walls mimic the grid of saplings that made up a *hale*'s underlying structure.

More importantly the building becomes a gateway to Ka Papa Lo'i 'O Kanewai, a traditional cultural garden where students grow *kalo* (taro), a sacred plant and staple of the Hawaiian diet. Discovered by a group of students, the *auw'ai* (irrigation ditch) that channels water to the *lo'i* from the nearby stream was dug hundreds of years ago as part of a once-vast network of waterways that supplied fresh water to the taro fields that dotted O'ahu's shores.

Twenty years later, few buildings have come close to achieving this balance of contemporary design and cultural history. With dozens of new buildings being added to the skyline, fierce debates have erupted around the phrase "a Hawaiian sense of place", which is intended as shorthand for design that is culturally and climatically appropriate to the islands. Many are dismayed by what they see as a superficial application of the concept: Hawaiian iconography decorating otherwise generic architecture. A fieldstone veneer here, a taro-leaf motif there.

Others have attempted to define Hawaiian architecture in less traditional but still appropriate ways, exemplified by projects such as the adaptive reuse of two historic airplane hangars for government offices on Ford Island and the rippling Waiea tower in Kaka'ako. The effort extends to the landscape too: like the *auwai* at Kanewai, a buried stream in Kaka'ako is being restored and made the centrepiece of a new public park.

We need buildings that truly embody a Hawaiian sense of place. But meandering through the *lo'i kalo* at Kanewai, watching minnows dart through the muddy water and studying the plants' wrinkled heart-shaped leaves, I think about how the taro leaf has become an icon – stamped on menus and T-shirts but also on our

**Modern buildings**
—
**01** Ka'iwakiloumoku Hawaiian Cultural Center
A contemporary take on traditional form and decor.
**02** Waiea Tower
Draws on ancient mythology while preparing for the future.
**03** Aulani Resort
Ersatz take on Hawaiian arts and crafts.

architecture – and how even our ugliest buildings might in some small way help sustain these symbols in the collective cultural memory.

If there is one thing that makes Honolulu unique, it is this: that a continuous, visible and still-vibrant thread stretches the length of the city's history. The thread is thin in places but it's there. What would other cities look like if indigenous practices were not just recognised but part of the collective memory and debated fiercely in the public realm? This is the question that the city asks of us, as well as the hope that it offers. The hope of continuity, of a past and people not forgotten. — (M)

**ABOUT THE WRITER:** Timothy A Schuler is a contributing editor at *Landscape Architecture Magazine* and writes about architecture, ecology and urban design. He lives in Honolulu.

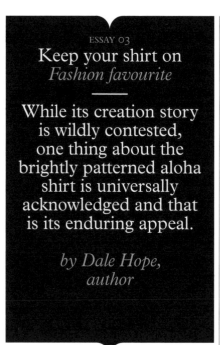

ESSAY 03
# Keep your shirt on
*Fashion favourite*

---

While its creation story is wildly contested, one thing about the brightly patterned aloha shirt is universally acknowledged and that is its enduring appeal.

*by Dale Hope,*
*author*

*"Adorned with romantic island motifs and tropical imagery, this casual attire reflects the wearer's encounters with a dreamy yet spirited tropical paradise"*

shirts to the campus. Made with narrow-width fabric, Young's shirts typically featured blue or black bamboo or geometric designs on a white background. They became quite the "topic of conversation", she said.

In 1984 an elderly woman called Margaret Young wrote to the editor of Hawaii's largest newspaper, the *Honolulu Star-Bulletin*, claiming she knew who had created the very first aloha shirt. She had recently read a new book, she said, that chronicled the history of Hawaii's most famous piece of clothing and it had jogged her memory: in the 1920s a classmate of hers at the University of Hawaii would come in wearing shirts made for him by his mother's dress-maker out of colourful *yukata* cloth, used by Japanese women for their work kimonos.

His name was Gordon Young – no relation, Margaret insisted – and he later began bringing consignments of his "new-style"

This is just one of countless stories about the creation of the aloha shirt; its true origins are still something of a contested question. Other versions of the tale argue that it is the happy result of colliding cultural influences from Japan, Hawaii and the mainland. Supporters of this theory point to the first-ever newspaper advert for an "aloha shirt", which appeared in June 1935. The advertiser was a Honolulu-based tailor called Musa-Shiya Shoten and the advert featured beautiful designs and radiant colours, "ready made or made to order 95 cents up".

The first trademark request for the term "aloha shirt" came in 1937 from clothing entrepreneur Ellery Chun. In a 1964 interview, Chun said that he had spotted local boys wearing casual shirts made of Japanese fabric and Filipino children wearing colourful *bayau* shirts. Inspired, he commissioned a tailor to make a batch of printed shirts out of gaudy Japanese kimono material. They were a hit and little handwritten signs for "Hawaiian shirts" soon began to appear in the windows of his father's clothing shop. It is here that the first ready-made aloha shirts hit the shelves.

The term "aloha shirt" is also contested and was once known, according to some, as the "Rathskellar shirt". The designer Rube Hauseman, another early producer of bright shirts, would dress his friends – the fabled Waikiki beach boys – in bold creations and tell them to go to the Rathskellar Bar, a favoured watering hole of Bing Crosby and other celebrities visiting from the mainland.

As the popularity of the aloha shirt grew, so too did the range of fabrics and patterns they were created with. "Men and Money at Work – Hawaii's Multi-Million Dollar Garment Industry", read a headline in the *Honolulu Star-Bulletin* in January 1953. The aloha shirt had become a homegrown industry: Japanese designs gradually gave way to

images of Hawaii; Mount Fuji was substituted with Diamond Head; and Japanese pine trees became coconut trees. Gone were the bamboo stalks, cranes, tigers and oriental shrines; in their place appeared thatched huts, ocean scenes and surfers, canoes on waves, tropical fish and native flowers.

Adorned with romantic island motifs and tropical imagery, this casual attire reflects the wearer's encounters with a dreamy yet spirited tropical paradise. Today, as in the 1930s, aloha shirts are worn after a day at the beach in Waikiki or to an evening luau. But they are also now commonly seen in boardrooms and the corridors of political power: the aloha shirt has woven its way into every corner of life here.

While its origins may never be definitively proven, modern Hawaii's best-known contribution to fashion continues to lend a dash of colour to notions of casual dress, both here and beyond our shores. Regardless of who is finally acknowledged as the shirt's creator, there is no mystery about its universal appeal. Architects like to say that "form follows function" and as such, the timeless aloha shirt – the sartorial symbol of our islands – allows us to wear our dreams on our sleeves. — (M)

**Popular designs**
──
**01 Bamboo**
Reportedly the first design to appear on an aloha shirt.
**02 Hawaiian flora**
Hawaiian tropical flowers were a staple from the 1960s.
**03 The Royal Hawaiian Hotel**
The Pink Palace on Waikiki Beach appears in several designs.

ABOUT THE WRITER: Dale Hope is the author of *The Aloha Shirt: The Spirit of The Islands*. He lives in Honolulu with his wife and daughter.

ESSAY 04
# A stroke of pluck
## *Making music*

---

The 1941 attack on Pearl Harbor had a devastating global impact but Kamaka, the maker of Hawaii's most instrumental cultural icon, emerged unscathed and is still thriving to this day.

*by Frederick Kamaka Sr, ukulele maker*

### Classic melodies

**01 He'eia**
Commemorating King Kalakaua's visit to the O'ahu surf spot of the same name.
**02 Susie Ana E**
Love song and favourite of late singer Genoa Keawe.
**03 Aloha 'Oe**
Most famous Queen Liluokalni composition.

At the time of the attack on Pearl Harbor – 7 December 1941 – my brother Sam Jr and I were apprentices at Kamaka and Sons, our father's ukulele workshop in Honolulu. Our father, Sam Kamaka, started the business in 1916 after spending five years in Europe learning the craft of making wooden instruments. Truthfully, he wanted to make guitars. But everyone in Hawaii was happy playing the ukulele – you could stick it under your arm and carry it around – so that's what he learned to make.

In 1926 he created his most famous instrument: a pineapple-shaped ukulele with a deep, rich sound. It set the standard that ukulele-makers all around the world strive for today. I'm very proud of that.

I was an eyewitness to the bombing. I was 17 years old and had enrolled at the military academy; I had a job at the diner and had to make sure everything was set up for lunch. On my way to the dining hall I stopped and stood where I usually did up on the heights. I looked to Waikiki and could see the sailboats. This was a little routine of mine: I would look towards Pearl Harbor to see if there were planes taking off from the Hickam airbase. That Sunday, there were no planes in the sky.

It was a clear day, with only one patch of clouds above the harbour. As I looked towards the mountains I saw a glint from the north, a light shining off what looked like metal and glass.

A week earlier the planes from Hickam had been practising manoeuvres and we had watched them do their exercises. So on that Sunday in December I thought this glint in the sky was a "V" formation.

One of my teachers from the academy walked past me, dressed in a suit for Sunday service. The next thing I knew I could see smoke and hear the noise of the bombs. "Sir, look," I said, "there's a bombing!" He looked at me and said, "Oh no, this is just part of the manoeuvres. They use dynamite to blow things up and generators to create smoke."

It took five or six minutes before there was any response from the ships. They were just shooting rounds into the air, hoping to hit something. Some of the rounds landed near the school and we were ordered to take cover in the basement. But then the USS *Arizona* blew up and the whole island shook. You

*"To be competitive you have to keep improving and experimenting"*

couldn't hold anyone inside the building after that: everybody went out to see it. The explosion stayed in the air for such a long time. At the time we had weapons but they didn't have firing pins. Right after the attack, we put them in.

When the war was just in Europe, people between the ages of 21 and 36 had to register and they might be called in to serve; after Pearl Harbor, they lowered the bar to 18. They enlisted all the guys from high school, everybody who was close to being that age. I was 17 but I was lucky. We lost many classmates; my class was cut by about 50 per cent.

Of course, life changes – and you have to accept it. What Sam and I knew when we grew up has long gone. There are now too many cars: everybody wants to have their own so the highways are crowded. And everything is more expensive. But there are also a lot more things to do: more restaurants and different recreational activities. People from all over the world have settled here and brought their culture with them.

Sam and I are now retired and our sons run the company, which is 100 years old. Every Kamaka ukulele is handcrafted and that is something that will never change – we build our instruments to last a lifetime – but our sons have brought the business into the modern era because to be competitive you have to keep improving and experimenting.

My father didn't want to stand still and neither did we; we hope our sons continue and pass the workshop on to the next generation. My father would be very proud of that – and so would I. — (M)

**ABOUT THE WRITER:** Frederick Kamaka Sr is the owner of the Kamaka Hawaii ukulele workshop, Hawaii's oldest ukulele manufacturer. Now in his nineties, he lives on the eastern side of O'ahu near his brother Sam, with whom he ran the company for 47 years.

ESSAY 05

# Attention Spam
*Slippery staple*

——

Ever since its arrival in the Second World War, Spam has stuck with Hawaii through thick and thin – and today, alongside fresh produce, it remains a favourite on Honolulu's culinary scene.

*by Martha Cheng*
*food writer*

If you don't like Spam, chances are you're eating it wrong. OK, admittedly it doesn't look particularly appetising: the pale-pink meat slides out of the can with a slurping sound, a gelatinous brick of meat slicked in glistening fat. But in Hawaii, Spam is still considered a staple – because we know how to make it delicious.

From diners and fast-food restaurants to the shelves of the nearest convenience store, Spam is ubiquitous in Hawaii. Launched in 1937 by Hormel Foods, it first arrived here during the Second World War when the US military sent canned non-perishable meat to the GIs stationed on the islands.

**Spam recipes**
—
**01 Spam musubi**
Wrap a strip of seaweed
around a slice of spam and a
narrow block of cooked rice.
**02 Spam fried rice**
Fry chunks of the pink stuff
with vegetables and rice.
**03 Spam chowder**
A traditional recipe with Spam
instead of clams.

It soon slipped into Hawaii's already eclectic food culture, which has been influenced by everyone from the Japanese, Chinese, Filipinos and South Koreans to the Portuguese labourers who arrived on the islands to work on the plantations.

For the non-believers I always recommend Spam musubi, a sure-fire hit guaranteed to make you a convert. Thickly slice a block of Spam and pan-fry it until some of the fat is rendered, the sides are browned and golden and the edges are slightly crispy – like perfectly cooked bacon. Place it on a slab of compact cooked rice and wrap it in a delicate sheet of nori. And there you have it: a Spam-inspired take on nigiri sushi.

It's sold everywhere, from 7-Eleven convenience stores across Honolulu to the higher-end Mana Bu snack-shop, which sells a variety of musubi lovingly packaged like little gifts. It is the perfect beach snack and the energy bar of choice for some hikers and even paddle-boarders, who cross the 51km of ocean between Moloka'i and O'ahu, refuelling on this convenient package of protein, salt and carbohydrates.

Spam musubi contributes considerably to Hawaii's startling consumption of this canned meat: some seven million cans are eaten here each year, more per capita than any other state in the US.

*"For the non-believers I always recommend Spam musubi, a sure-fire hit guaranteed to make you a convert"*

It also finds its way into fried rice and *saimin* (a Hawaiian noodle soup), as well as onto breakfast plates: Spam, eggs and rice is a particularly popular way for many to start the day.

And then there are the weirder and more creative combinations that come out every spring for Waikiki's annual Spam Jam, one of Hawaii's most popular food festivals. Here you might see a Spam and *ahi katsu* (Spam and raw tuna wrapped in seaweed and flash-fried), Spam fries, Spam cupcakes and even chunks of Spam folded into a macnut-brittle iced lolly for dessert.

But there are many of us who wish Hawaii could quell its appetite for Spam, who want these islands to be known for the chefs who use Hawaii's fresh produce and fish, for the restaurants listed in this guide.

In recent years a new wave of culinary energy has flooded Honolulu: we are honouring native Hawaiian food in new ways and paying homage to Hawaii's plantation culture, all the while incorporating new influences and ideas into our menus.

So why does Spam still stick around? For the same reason that Honolulu still has so many hole-in-the-wall restaurants and half-a-century-old diners tucked away in all corners of the city. These places and the food they serve are the keepers of our memories. They are a part of what makes Honolulu. — (M)

ESSAY 06

## The King and I
*Hawaii's main man*

——

'Aloha from Hawaii via Satellite' cemented Elvis's love affair with Honolulu and was the biggest spectacle in TV history. Take a tour and you'll see he hasn't left the city, let alone the building.

*by Jerry Hopkins, writer*

Just before midnight on 14 January 1973, Elvis Presley took to the stage at the Honolulu International Center for what would be one of the defining concerts of his career and, at the time, the most expensive television event ever staged.

*Aloha from Hawaii via Satellite* was the first live performance in entertainment history to be broadcast worldwide by satellite. Inspiration for the show struck Elvis's manager Colonel Tom Parker when he saw President Nixon live by satellite reopening relations with China in 1971. "If Nixon can do it," he said, "Elvis can do it too."

Legendary television director Marty Pasetta, who had found fame in the business for his work on the Academy Awards ceremonies, was brought on board to bring the spectacle to the world. With a budget of about $2.5m, no expense was spared. Pasetta transformed the venue, covering nearly half of the arena's 8,000 seats, enlarging the stage and dotting huge

ABOUT THE WRITER: Martha Cheng is a freelance food writer and editor based in Honolulu. She is a former line cook and food-truck owner; the latter, incidentally, didn't serve Spam at all.

*"The feeling for many Hawaiians remains mutual: to many, Elvis is still the last Hawaiian king"*

neon signs around the arena that read "We Love Elvis" in seven languages.

The run-up to the event wasn't without the odd difficulty. Elvis, in a moment of spontaneous generosity that caused no small headache for his dressers, gave away his bejewelled belt to Jack Lord, star of the wildly popular *Hawaii Five-O* cop show. "But we've used all the rubies!" said designer Bill Belew, when he was told to send a replacement belt from Los Angeles. On the day there were technical problems too: no single event in Honolulu had ever required so much electrical equipment, and it drained the power supply.

The performance, however, began without a hitch at midnight Hawaii time, ensuring that it would go out primetime to Australia and Asia, including to GIs in Vietnam. The following night it was rebroadcast in 28 European countries via simulcast and later by NBC in the US. The Colonel modestly claimed an audience of 1.5 billion worldwide.

Elvis performed concerts in Honolulu in each of the three decades his career spanned from the 1950s, a record that no other non-Hawaiian performer has matched – or likely ever will. Over the years he continually holidayed in Hawaii, sometimes with a female companion and sometimes not but always with his gang of roughhousing friends known as the Memphis Mafia. He took his final holiday here five months before he died in 1977.

Sites associated with the King can still be visited today and have become something of a pilgrimage for fans from around the world. The colourful Rainbow Tower at Waikiki's Hilton Hawaiian Village resort is one; Elvis stayed here in 1957 on his first visit to the islands and returned 16 years later for the *Aloha from Hawaii* concert. Other points on the Elvis trail in Honolulu include the venue for *Aloha from*

**Places to pay homage to the King**

**01 Elvis Aloha statue**
Life-sized bronze statue at the Neal S Blaisdell Center.
**02 Hilton Hawaiian Village**
Suites at the Rainbow Tower hosted Elvis and his entourage.
**03 Mount Tantalus**
One of the locations for *Blue Hawaii* (1961).

*Hawaii*, now the Neal S Blaisdell Center. The life-sized statue of Elvis near the box office is forever adorned with flower lei left behind by visiting fans.

In *Paradise, Hawaiian Style* Elvis sang at the Polynesian Cultural Center and frolicked at Hanauma Bay. In *Girls, Girls, Girls* he tied up his charter boat at Kewalo Basin. In *Blue Hawaii* there were scenes filmed at Waikiki Beach, Ala Moana Park and the Punchbowl crater. But it is perhaps *Aloha from Hawaii via Satellite* that cemented Hawaii's place in Elvis's affections. The feeling for many Hawaiians remains mutual: to many, Elvis is still the last Hawaiian king.

Elvis shopped at normal hours, sunbathed and played football on a public beach. On his final holiday in Honolulu, in a small mall near the beach house he had leased, he spontaneously paid the bill for a stranger while buying gifts to take back to Memphis. He liked Hawaii because the islands' residents didn't hassle him; it may have been the only place where he could appear publicly without causing a fuss. No wonder there are those who say he's sometimes seen at the Manoa Marketplace grocery shop even to this day. — (M)

**ABOUT THE WRITER:** Jerry Hopkins is a journalist and author, best known for writing the first comprehensive biography of Elvis Presley, *Elvis*, published in 1971. He is a former contributing editor to *Rolling Stone* magazine and he lives in Thailand.

# Small gains
## *State of the art*

Honolulu's lack of space is not indicative of its artistic reach. In fact, it's the island's close quarters that make for such a fertile breeding ground for creativity.

*by Pegge Hopper, painter and gallerist*

There is an intimacy to Hawaii and its art world rarely found elsewhere. Perhaps this is due in part to the state's small population and limited number of square miles, which inevitably lead to overlapping relationships and artistic inspirations. Influenced by the family bonds that are such an important part of life here, ours is an artistic community that nurtures even as it makes its way in a competitive art world beyond Hawaii's shores.

While paradise here is certainly not lost, Hawaii has been the site of many trials throughout its history. Art has thrived because of the underlying toughness that exists on the islands – a resilience that is rarely acknowledged. All this lushness is growing out of lava rock, after all.

It is significant then that women and minorities vibrantly represent modern art in Hawaii, not simply as subjects but as artists, directors and tastemakers. It has been this way since the beginning, even when the role of women was more restricted and the opportunities more meagre.

When I arrived in 1963 I found a nurturing and lushly organic Hawaii but not the untouched tropical relic it is often marketed as. I have never depicted the islands or the people here as a fairytale. The women in my paintings, I hope, bear little resemblance to the stereotypical hula girl who has become one of the most familiar parts of our visual vocabulary.

The women in my work are distant but not exotic. They are people you almost know, who you think you have met before. I have always wanted to capture women as sublimely indifferent to their audience, looking inward and existing only for themselves.

When visitors come to my gallery they ask about my models:

### Hawaiian artists

**01 Cornelia MacIntyre Foley**
Famous for her portraits of voluptuous Hawaiian women.
**02 William Twigg-Smith**
New Zealand-born painter who worked mainly in Hawaii.
**03 Isami Doi**
Printmaker and painter with work in the Honolulu Museum of Art.

who they are, where they come from. I tell them I don't know. I like to keep my distance from the women I paint, whose privacy has historically been encroached upon.

I have lived here almost all my life but I am aware that to be *kama'aina* (local) is not the same as being a native Hawaiian. In that, I am still a respectful outsider. When I first arrived in Honolulu I went to the state archives and leafed through the collections of photographs of native women there. The women were either caring for their children, strumming ukuleles or greeting fishing boats as they landed on the beaches. I had recently become a mother myself and the nostalgia and romance in the photographs captivated me. I began to paint them.

Soon after, my first commission came: it was from the influential interior designer Mary Philpotts, who was renovating the Kona Villages resort. I created 22 paintings for her – using the striking colour-blocking my work would later become known for – and by 1983 I had opened my own gallery in the city's historic Chinatown.

In 2011, when the tsunami hit Kona island, the Kona Village resort was destroyed. When I saw the destruction on television I assumed that my paintings had been washed away with it.

However, this past winter my gallery received a phone call. A consignment store had discovered the 22 paintings that I had created

*"Ours is an artistic community that nurtures even as it makes its way in a competitive art world"*

more than 30 years ago. In the confusion that followed the tsunami, the consignment store-owner said the canvases were stacked on the shelves of a forgotten storage unit that the owner had recently bought.

After the hotel works I began to be commissioned not just by individuals but also by museums and organisations. My favourite piece is my "Lahainaluna", which I painted for the anniversary of Lahainaluna High School in Maui, the oldest high school west of the Rocky Mountains. The original – earthier and less composed than the finished work – hangs in my room today.

I thrived on these commissions because they exposed me to a wider audience and gave me a chance to be involved in the community of Chinatown, which has become the city's artistic core. It is through here that much of Hawaii's creative output flows: artists come and go; galleries open and close.

Art isn't confined to the galleries either: the lack of space here often leads to the reinvention of familiar places in ways that surprise and delight. The Manifest coffee house on Hotel Street, which doubles as a whisky bar and music venue at night, regularly hosts receptions and exhibitions for emerging artists. Similarly, every first Friday of the month, the Ong King Arts Center on King Street allows performance artists to workshop their pieces to an audience.

While it was still gaining legitimacy elsewhere, graffiti art flourished here early on and led to the Pow! Wow! gathering. Held every February, this event invites both local and international artists to create murals in Kaka'ako, a former industrial area of Honolulu.

The traditional arts in Hawaii – from koa woodworking to lei floristry – are experiencing something of a renaissance. And like those traditional crafts, the contemporary arts in Hawaii have never stagnated. The first Honolulu Biennial will take place in 2017, a flourish on the long path that these islands and their artists have trodden to become a contemporary cultural capital in a remote patch of the Pacific.

I am grateful to have been embraced here, where I found my feet as an artist, a businesswoman and a mother. Honolulu was fertile ground for me and it continues to be so, which is why perhaps, now in my eighties, I continue to work, create and paint. — (M)

ABOUT THE WRITER: Pegge Hopper is a painter and gallerist. The Honolulu art gallery that bears her name is one of Chinatown's longest-standing contemporary-art galleries. Her work can be found in private collections around the world.

ESSAY 08
# Making waves
*Surf's up*
───

**With its warm waters and quality swells – not to mention the presence of watersports masters the Waikiki beach boys – Hawaii is the perfect place to dip a toe into the ocean.**

*by Laura Blears,
former professional surfer*

Surfing has always been a part of my life. Riding a wave, flowing with the moving ocean, the current under your board as you curve this way and that like a dance; the feeling is amazing.

My family moved to Hawaii from California in 1956 and I started surfing at beautiful Waikiki Beach when I was six years old. My father, Lord James Blears, was a professional wrestler and a surfer.

We moved into an old two-storey apartment by the beach on Kalakaua Avenue and there was a surf shop on the ground floor. It was a wonderful place to live: we only had to walk down the steps to the street and within a few moments we were in the warm, blue waters of the ocean. It was the most awesome place to grow up: swimming in the sea every day, riding the waves and feeling free.

The first time I stood on a surfboard, my father was with me. I remember getting up on the board and him pushing me out into the waves. I stood up and rode the

*"In some places the waves are hollow, in others they tower above you; there is always a challenge once you hit the water"*

waters all the way to the beach, where my mother was waiting for me on the sand.

My career in surfing really began at this young age. We were always surfing, swimming and paddling in the canoe with the Waikiki beach boys when they took visitors out for rides. My dad would enter my brother and me in the children's paddle-board competitions; even back then I was competing against the boys.

I became the first female professional surfer in 1972 at the Smirnoff Pro surfing competition on the north shore of Oʻahu. The following year I was asked to compete as an "alternate" and surf against the men.

In the first round of the competition I felt nervous but quietly confident. I beat one man in that heat but didn't advance after that. But that was just the beginning for me. The following year the sponsors held a competition for six women: a winner-takes-all contest at Sunset Beach on the North Shore. I won and was given a cheque and the title of surfing's first female professional. I couldn't believe it.

One competition that stands out for me was winning the Makaha International Surfing Championship on the west coast of Oʻahu, which was considered by many to be the unofficial world championship between 1954 and 1971. I didn't have my own board so I borrowed one of Dennis Pang's, the best surfboard-maker in Hawaii. Being on that board was like riding on a magic carpet.

The waves that day were wonderful and the ocean fresh and blue; the conditions were perfect. I remember sliding down those walls of water, making a bottom turn and another turn and kicking out the other side and then winning.

There were challenges when I began competing because the men always got to start; it took a long time for women to get to the same position. Today, however, women are right up there and I feel I paved the way a little. We are now where we are meant to be.

Hawaii is one of the best locations in the world to surf. We have a great water temperature here and the swells in several areas make for perfect surfing spots. In some places the waves are hollow, in others they tower above you; there is always a challenge once you hit the water.

There is one wave that will always stick in my memory. I was the first person to do a hula-hoop on the shoulders of one of the Waikiki beach boys who was riding the waves in Waikiki. What a feeling. It made the front page of the local newspaper.

I still surf today and have taught my son the sport, like my parents taught me. The sea is now a playground for my granddaughter too. When I see her on her little board I feel like surfing has come full circle for me.

Hawaii still has its magic: the Hawaiian people are full of aloha and kindness and have big hearts. But when you are alone on your board on the ocean, with the feel of the spray and the fresh air on your skin, your thoughts are focused on the movement of the water beneath you. You just have that feeling of being free. — (M)

**ABOUT THE WRITER:** Laura Blears is a former professional surfer and the first female professional in the sport. Her brother Jimmy was crowned world surfing champion in 1972. She currently lives on Maui.

ESSAY 09

# Pulling the strings
*Guitar hero*

——

From the 1830s to the present day the quiet, melancholic strum of the slack-key guitar has threaded its way through Hawaii's music scene.

*by George Kahumoku Jr, slack-key guitarist*

I was born into a big musical family: 26 cousins, a dozen aunties and uncles, two sets of grandparents and great-grandparents all shared the same household in Kealia on South Kona island. We were a family of fishermen, farmers and cowboys and our life was remote. We didn't have a TV or radio reception so we learned about Hawaiian culture by entertaining ourselves. Together we told stories, played music, sang songs and danced the hula.

I began playing the slack-key ukulele at the age of three. When I was nine and my fingers were big enough my cousins and grandfather taught me how to play the slack-key guitar. Our home was the party house of the village. My grandfather Willy was a pig farmer so we owned the only *imu* (outdoor oven) in our community. For special celebrations – birthdays, marriages and deaths, as well as house and canoe-warmings – people would come to buy pigs from us and roast them in our oven. There would be parties before and after the festivities and we would eat, sing and play the guitar, our music filling the air.

The history of the slack-key guitar in Hawaii has become a fable of sorts for those of us who play it today. In the 1830s, groups of *vaquero* (Hispanic horse-mounted livestock herders) arrived to tame the cattle that had been introduced to our islands in 1793 by English explorer George Vancouver. By day the *vaquero* taught the Hawaiians to manage the cows and by night they taught us how to play the guitar around the campfires. The *vaquero* had three types of guitar: a four-string that played the bass; a six-string used to set the rhythm; and another four-string to pick out the lead melody. It's this

**Slack-key albums**
——
01 **Pure Gabby**
Recording of the slack-key master Gabby Pahinui.
02 **Nahenahe – Hawaiian Slack Key**
A classic by George Kuo; the title refers to a soothing style.
03 **Makana**
Debut album by guitarist and singer Makana.

*"The way we play and the sound the slack-key creates is influenced by our tropical environment and our connection to the land, sea and each other"*

As such, the Hawaiians removed the strings and restrung the guitar frames but left the strings slack and the slack-key – or *kiho'alu*, as we say in Hawaiian – was born. My great-great-grandfather, incidentally, was one of the Hawaiians who received one of those original guitars, left behind by the *vaquero*.

When I play my guitar today I imagine all my family playing with me, even if I'm performing solo. I feel the spirit of the song, the place I'm singing about – something we call *wahi pana* in Hawaiian. I can hear and recall the aloha and the spirit that the song evokes when I sing. The songs of the past remind me of the days of my youth when my *kupuna* (forebears) sang these same melodies to me.

What makes the slack-key unique is that it allows us to play bass, rhythm and lead all in a slackened or open tuning. For me, the way we play and the sound the

combination of instruments that is still used by many Mariachi bands in Mexico today.

When the *vaquero* left the islands in the early 1830s they left behind a few guitars but didn't share their tunings.

slack-key creates is influenced by our tropical environment and our connection to the land, sea and each other. There is something meditative about the sound of the slack-key: it soothes the soul, no matter where you come from. It captures and emulates our sense of place and the "live and let live" approach that we hold dear here on the islands.

When I was growing up we knew all our neighbours and we were connected by a sense of community. We shared each other's cultures and, in my memories at least, it's the sound of the slack-key that wove it all together.

Music, growing one's own food, hunting, fishing, sharing and celebrating: these are the things that help us connect with one another. Music has given me so many opportunities and has taken me to 55 countries around the world. I know how blessed I am to come from and live in a place of abundance, a place that my ancestors helped create. Now it is my turn to share what has been shared with me. — (M)

ABOUT THE WRITER: George Kahumoku Jr is a Grammy award-winning slack-key guitarist and a grandee of the genre in Hawaii. He regularly performs across the state, often with his wife Nancy (who dances hula). When not performing, he harvests guavas and herds goats on his ranch on Maui.

ESSAY 10
# Gift of the gab
*Literary legacy*

———

Much has been written about Honolulu, by both locals and tourists – among the latter, Robert Louis Stevenson. It's the island's oral tradition, however, that first introduced the idea of telling stories and encouraged us to listen.

*by Stephanie Han, teacher and writer*

My uncle Howard is the oral chronicler of family lore: he remembers standing on the rooftop of his home in Kunia Camp, the pineapple plantation off the red dirt road, waving innocently at the squadron of Japanese Zeros flying low overhead on their way to bomb Pearl Harbor.

It could be the size of the island or that we're all on The Rock in the Pacific but it seems like there's an understanding that memories link people. In Hawaii you frequently bump into the past; everyone knows someone who can make a personal connection to happenings such as a tidal wave ("Big one, way up the street in Hilo!") or Queen Lili'uokalani's reign ("Your grandma saw her funeral parade").

In Hawaii we have a phrase – "talk story" – that roughly means to chat, gossip or tell a tale. To talk story is to recount history, affirm bonds and assert the right to laugh, honour and listen. The islands' oral tradition is often delivered in Pidgin English, a language that built a local identity and continues to unite a community with linguistic differences. Talk story is one of Hawaii's arts and it played a role in Honolulu's stature as a Pacific literary hub.

Where better to explore an idea of paradise on earth, real or imagined? The city has evolved from the O'ahu 1866 harbour town that Mark Twain declared as "high, rugged, useless, barren, black and dreary" to a million-strong metropolis. It boasts a literary pedigree of luminaries who stoke the city's volcanic myths that still linger in the air long after the whaling ships and women on horseback have given way to traffic jams of tourists in rental cars.

It's impossible to sum up a single idea of writerly discovery here because what you find is Hawaii itself: it is its own definition.

Robert Louis Stevenson stayed on Kaimana Beach (or Sans Souci), talking story with other guests under the hau tree that still shades a beachside café *lanai* (veranda). He was received by King Kalakaua at 'Iolani Palace and befriended his half-Scottish niece Princess Victoria Ka'iulani, composing a poem for her before she went to school in England.

He wrote in the hotel register: "If anyone desires such old-fashioned things as lovely scenery, quiet pure air, clear sea water, good food and heavenly sunsets hung out before their eyes over the Pacific and the distant hills of Waiana, I recommend him cordially to the 'Sans Souci'." The intrepid can find Stevenson's beach shack on display at Manoa's Waioli Tea Room, up the stairs from a well featured in Elvis Presley's *Blue Hawaii*.

The 20th century saw the arrival of a fictionalised Hawaii. Jack London and Somerset Maugham penned missives and stories that told uncomfortable truths and spun

*"It's impossible to sum up a single idea of writerly discovery here because what you find is Hawaii itself: it is its own definition"*

romanticised visions of life in the Pacific. Earl Derr Biggers wrote *The House Without a Key* (1925), modelled on Chinese-Hawaiian detective Chang Apana, while staying at what is now the Halekulani hotel.

The mainland's infatuation with Hawaii began in the run up to statehood in 1959. Paradise could be found within the country's borders, amplifying a tropical iteration of the American Dream. James Michener's epic *Hawaii* (1959) solidified a now dated but highly influential image of Hawaii in the US imagination and his legacy here is punctuated by a donation of more than 5,000 Japanese ukiyo-e prints to the Honolulu Academy of Art.

Joan Didion's essay on Honolulu in *The White Album* (1979) juxtaposed her personal narrative with Honolulu's iconic setting. She waited to see a tidal wave set to hit the shores on TV while contemplating her own: "We are here on this island in the middle of the Pacific in lieu of filing for divorce." She was unaware that voices outside the pink Royal Hawaiian Hotel would forever change Honolulu's literature.

It would no longer be a literature written exclusively by those outside of the islands. It would be told by those born and raised here, or those who dared to claim it as home.

To understand Hawaii's brutal past, read the work of Haunani Kay-Trask, a writer and leader of the native Hawaiian movement. Maxine Hong Kingston spent years teaching in Honolulu and in *Hawaii One Summer* (1987) she describes Mokoli'i, an islet formerly known as Chinaman's Hat,

and the blue of Kane'ohe Bay. She ponders the questions of land, belonging and nature that continue to surface as Hawaii grapples with its past while facing the future.

Local writers Milton Murayama and Cathy Song descend from the Japanese, Chinese and Korean plantation workers who revealed the complications of the halcyon escape sold to tourists. Murayama's portrait of a Japanese-US family prior to the Second World War and his rendering of Pidgin English readable to natives and outsiders alike was a literary first. Song's poetry reveals a life that has recently disappeared, the last sugar plantation announcing its closure in 2016. The Waipahu Plantation Village offers a glimpse of a world far from the glittery stretch of Waikiki.

Writing differs from talk story and to ensure the past's record, Uncle Howard briefly functioned as family scribe. I read about my late grandmother, the archetypal Virginia Slims-smoking woman, defying her family by becoming a nurse. She ran crying from the house down Punchbowl Street to stay at the YWCA, an elegant structure designed by Julia Morgan. As I think about my grandmother, my uncle smiles and says: "That YWCA was where I dumped a live shark in the pool to surprise my girlfriend who was living in the dorms!" Talk story.

Talk story lives in that it is an individualistic act of defiance against the stories told and taught by outsiders and authorities. The tradition contributed to a tacit understanding shared among writers on the islands, which is this: we no longer assume that a single narrative about Hawaii exists. We acknowledge it as a place of multiplicity and myth, a place of many strands and stars. Hawaii is densely packed history, an endless ocean of words and the tales that everyone holds in their hearts: the story that has yet to hit the page. — (M)

**ABOUT THE WRITER:** Stephanie Han is an award-winning writer of fiction; her debut short-story collection *Swimming in Hong Kong* will be published in 2016. Her family has lived in Hawaii since 1904.

ESSAY II
# Song and dance
*All hail hula*

Hula is one of Hawaii's oldest traditions and – recalling the history and culture of the islands alongside a song – it's about much more than moving your feet.

*by Skyler Kamaka, hula dancer*

I began dancing hula at the age of five and it has always been a part of me: I have hula in my blood. My great-grandmother was a *kumu hula* (hula teacher) and my great-grandfather started our family-run ukulele business Kamaka Hawaii in 1916. All of my aunts and uncles are either musicians or hula dancers so our family gatherings are always filled with song and dance.

Hula is an interpretive dance; every movement represents a part of our story, either literally or figuratively depending on the *kauna* (hidden meaning) of the *mele* (song). The more traditional version is Hula Kahiko, performed to the beat of a *pahu* (drum) or *ipu heke* (a gourd percussion instrument). With the westernisation of Hawaii and the arrival of string instruments in the 19th century, a modern style called Hula 'Auana then came about.

Hawaiian *mele* are poetic; they talk of Hawaii's history and the beauty of the land. One of my favourites to dance to is a love song called "Ke Aloha", written by Lei Collins and composed by Maddy K Lam. This *mele* is written from one lover to another; the main character shares her feelings towards her beloved and sings of the affection she feels when the two of them are together. It's a traditional Hawaiian song that people dance to at most luaus and family gatherings.

At one point the hula, along with our language, was banned here. The dwindling number of cultural practitioners, along with the increase of western influences, pushed Hawaiian culture to the brink of extinction. However, it has survived and so have we who practise it.

Although there are few master practitioners alive today, I've been taught by some great *kumu hulas*. I learned my first hula, "Little Brown Gal", from my great-aunt Laila

### Hula steps

**01 'Ami**
A core hula move, rotating your hips gently to the left and right.
**02 Huli**
Turn around slowly while swaying the hips.
**03 Kaholo**
A sliding step, used to move from side to side, front to back or diagonally.

*"Hula is an interpretive dance; every movement represents a part of our story"*

Riplenger, a famous dancer in the 1930s. This simple song is a classic *hapa haole* tune, which means it's sung in English but set to Hawaiian music. It says, "It's not the islands fair that are calling to me, it's not the balmy air or the tropical sea. It's a little brown gal in a little grass skirt, in a little grass shack in Hawaii."

Hula has taken me around the world and given me the chance to dance for a variety of dignitaries. My favourite performance was at the finale of Miss America 2013; I was Miss Hawaii. I performed "Poli'ahu", a song written for the snow goddess Poli'ahu, who lives at the summit of Mauna Kea on the Big Island. It talks about Poli'ahu calling out to her lover across the sea.

"Poli'ahu" has a haunting melody that captivates the audience – and it enchants me too. Dancing to that song at the Miss America pageant was a beautiful moment for me. I felt I was sharing the love of my culture and family on a national stage. I was very proud. — (M)

ABOUT THE WRITER: Skyler Kamaka is a hula dancer at House Without a Key, the Halekulani Hotel's legendary bar. She hosts the *HiSessions* music television programme and was crowned Miss Hawaii in 2012. She is also a pilot for the Hawaii Air National Guard.

ESSAY 12
# Hitting a home run
*A jogger's tour*

**Running in Honolulu is a great way to discover how the city has grown from a small town into a modern metropolis with a unique culture and diverse populace.**

*by David Y Ige, governor of Hawaii*

I'm an avid jogger. Always have been. There was a time when I would enter the occasional 5km or 10km race but these days I jog mostly for exercise.

One exception is the annual Great Aloha Run, a road race for charity and a wonderful Hawaii tradition. On 15 February 2016 my wife Dawn and I joined more than 24,000 runners, joggers and walkers on the 13km route from the landmark Aloha Tower in downtown Honolulu to Aloha Stadium near Pearl Harbor.

Most mornings I jog alone – that is, if you don't count my security detail. My route rewards me with a captivating view of the city's small-town roots and its rise as a modern, cosmopolitan Pacific metropolis.

I set off early, often before sunrise, departing from the governor's residence next door to Washington Place on Beretania Street. A tour of the stately mansion, built in 1847, is a superb opportunity to learn about Honolulu's history, dating back to a time when travel to Hawaii was only by ship.

Across the street from Washington Place is the Hawaii State Capitol, where our elected officials (myself included) serve the people. This impressive structure, whose architecture symbolises Hawaii's natural elements, was built in 1969 and is open weekdays for self-guided tours. Be sure to visit Room 415 for visitor information.

On the opposite side of the capitol, fronting King Street, is 'Iolani Palace. Once the home of Hawaii's ruling monarchy, it is the only royal palace on US soil and a must-see for visitors. The stories of its architecture and artefacts provide a rich history of a royal home that for decades served as the centrepiece of Honolulu.

Across from 'Iolani Palace is a building you'll recognise if you're a fan of the TV series *Hawaii Five-O*. Although known to viewers as the HQ of Lt Commander Steve McGarrett and his Five-O police force, in reality it is Ali'iolani Hale, meeting place of the Supreme Court of Hawaii. A tour offers an overview of Hawaii's legal history.

Jogging east on King Street I look up at Kawaiaha'o Church, often referred to as the "Westminster Abbey of Hawaii". Dedicated in 1842, this dignified structure made of coral carved from ocean reefs is a much-revered witness of the passage of time from old to modern Hawaii.

On land adjoining the church are the Hawaiian mission houses, which offer a glimpse into the lives of 7's first Christian missionaries following their arrival in Honolulu in 1820. The site features three restored structures, two of which are the

*"The routes are enlightening in their visual storytelling of the beginnings and growth of the city of Honolulu and state of Hawaii"*

oldest houses still standing in their original locations.

Just across the street from these historic landmarks on King Street is Honolulu Hale, the official seat of government for the City and County of Honolulu, led by my good friend, mayor Kirk Caldwell. Beautifully landscaped and well kept, the Civic Center grounds surrounding Honolulu Hale are ideal for jogging or walking, as well as picnics and gatherings.

When I jog through this section of downtown Honolulu I see the foundations of a close-knit community that rose to become a modern city. It is a city that grew without sacrificing the very best qualities of small-town life. A city where each succeeding generation continues to respect the past while welcoming the future.

Of course there are many other wonderful places in Honolulu to see while jogging. Before I was elected governor I had a favourite 8km route that looped through the Pearl City and Aiea neighbourhoods near my family home.

Since moving to the governor's residence in downtown Honolulu I've developed some new favourites. The routes are enlightening in their visual storytelling of the beginnings and growth of the city of Honolulu and state of Hawaii, with structures that are admired as treasures for their perpetuation of our history.

On your next visit to Hawaii take time to see the historic Honolulu sites on my jogging route. And if you happen to pass a jogger accompanied by a security detail, be sure to give me a wave. — (M)

**Hawaii politicians**
—
**01 Daniel Inouye**
Hawaii's first congressman after statehood in 1959 and a long-serving US senator.
**02 General Erik K Shinseki**
The first Hawaiian to be made Chief of Staff of the US army.
**03 Eileen Anderson**
The only woman to be elected mayor of Honolulu.

**ABOUT THE WRITER:** David Y Ige was elected governor of Hawaii in November 2014. Born and raised in Pearl City on the island of O'ahu, he entered politics in 1985, serving in the Hawaii House of Representatives for 10 years and then in the Hawaii State Senate from 1995.

# Culture
## —— Blurred lines

The 1950s Hollywood version of Hawaii had swaying hula girls, ukulele strummers, aloha shirts and extravagant sunsets. You'll still find all of those in 21st-century Honolulu but the city's arts scene is far more diverse, with musicians, writers, painters, publishers and designers re-examining and reinterpreting what it means to be Hawaiian.

It's what you would expect of a place where migrants from Polynesia, Portugal, Japan, China, South Korea, the Philippines, Vietnam and beyond have settled for generations and where distinctions between these cultures have become blurred over time. For such a small remote city, Honolulu has a surprising range of world-class museums and thriving independent publishers, not to mention a nascent fashion industry. And the music and dance will leave as lasting an impression on you as the palm trees, sunshine and sea breeze.

① 
Spalding House,
Tantalus-Makiki Heights
*Artful setting*

Spalding House was the home of Anna Rice Cooke, founder of the Honolulu Museum of Art (*see page 88*); it became an annexe of the museum in 2011. The beautiful residence was designed in 1925 by architect Hart Wood and occupies a plum spot with views over Honolulu. The garden, created between 1928 and 1941, is known as *Nu'umealani*, meaning "heavenly terrace". There are five main galleries, sculptures in the garden and a café, plus a pavilion for David Hockney's sets for Ravel's opera, *L'Enfant et les Sortilèges*.
*2411 Makiki Heights Drive*
*+1 808 526 1322*
*honolulumuseum.org*

Mixed media
Lose yourself in this eclectic museum

② 
Honolulu Museum of Art, Makiki
*Eclectic collection*

New York architect Bertram Goodhue used a host of materials in the construction of this exceptional art museum, from Oʻahu's volcanic rock to Chinese granite that arrived in Hawaii as ballast for ships transporting the island's sandalwood. A stroll through the museum – the largest of its kind in Hawaii – provides a welcome respite from the heat and bustle of Honolulu.

With 50,000 pieces spanning 5,000 years, there is something for everyone here: the broad collection ranges from medieval altarpieces to landscape paintings. The museum is especially strong on Asian art and has 10,000 Japanese woodblock prints. Since opening in 1927 there have been numerous additions to the building, including the 280-seat Doris Duke Theatre in 1977, a gift shop (*see page 54*) and a café. The museum is closed on Mondays.
*900 South Beretania Street*
*+1 808 532 8700*
*honolulumuseum.org*

**First Fridays**

Once down at heel, Chinatown today is brimming with bars, shops and galleries. The neighbourhood springs to life on the first Friday of every month. Join the evening art walk to meet gallerists and artists in venues such as Arts at Marks Garage and the Pegge Hopper Gallery.
*firstfridayhawaii.com*

③

**Bernice Pauahi Bishop Museum, Kalihi**
*Island records*

Named after Princess Bernice Pauahi Bishop, great-granddaughter of King Kamehameha I, the Bishop houses the largest collection of Hawaiian artefacts in the world. Among its 1.2 million cultural objects are Kamehameha's cape and a board belonging to surfing great Duke Kahanamoku.

The display, which puts Hawaii into a broader Pacific context, runs from pre-contact to the present day and sensitively navigates the issues around Hawaii's annexation by the US in 1898. The 19th-century halls have been given an overhaul, allowing the old koa wood to shine again, while the bookshop is a must for anyone interested in ethnography, language or natural history. Its selection of titles complement gift-shop staples such as lauhala hats handwoven from the native hala tree.
*1525 Bernice Street*
*+1 808 847 3511*
*bishopmuseum.org*

④
**ʻIolani Palace, Downtown**
*Fit for a king*

ʻIolani was built in 1882 as the official residence of King Kalakaua and his successor, Queen Liliʻuokalani; however, it was only in use for a decade before the monarchy was overthrown in 1893. Several architects had a hand in the elaborate "American Florentine" design, brought to life by contractors using wood from the Pacific Northwest, glass doors from San Francisco and an array of Hawaiian woods such as koa, kou and kamani for the ornate interior woodwork. King Kalakaua, ever one for innovation, installed electric lights and telephones.

Old photographs reveal an interior stuffed with sofas and paintings; although more sparsely furnished today, rooms such as the library and the state dining room hint at the life of the king and queen. The palace served as a government building until 1969 when the adjacent Hawaii State Capitol (*see page 100*) was completed; it reopened as a museum in 1978. Guided or audio tours are available and The Royal Hawaiian Band (*see page 93*) plays here on Friday afternoons.
*364 South King Street*
*+1 808 522 0832*
*iolanipalace.org*

⑤
**Honolulu Museum of Art at First Hawaiian Center, Downtown**
*Bank of art*

This downtown outpost of the Honolulu Museum of Art (*see*

*opposite*) opened in 1996 and showcases work by emerging artists. The building – the tallest on the islands – also houses the headquarters of the First Hawaiian Bank. It was designed by mega-structure architecture firm Kohn Pedersen Fox (the creators of such contemporary icons as the Shanghai World Financial Center). Entry is free and the museum is open during banking hours.
*999 Bishop Street*
*+808 532 8701*
*honolulumuseum.org*

⑥
**Hawaii State Art Museum, Downtown**
*Art for all*

Hawaii was the first state to adopt the "Per Cent for Art" law in 1967, which means that 1 per cent of state building construction costs go towards funding public works of art. The collection runs to 7,000 works. Five hundred are on the walls of hospitals, schools and airports but many are on display here for free, including contemporary pieces by Hawaiian artists such as Miki Nitadori and Kauaʻi ceramicist David Kuraoka. The Spanish-mission-style building dates back to 1927.
*2f, 250 South Hotel Street*
*+1 808 586 0900*
*sfca.hawaii.gov*

## Theatre and film
Curtain up

①
Hawaii Theatre Center, Chinatown
*Restoration drama*

When this venue opened in 1922
as Honolulu's newest cultural
institution, it was described as the
perfect theatre. Its architecture
was a marvel, melding neoclassical
design with art deco aesthetic, while
the 1,350-seat auditorium offered
views unimpeded by columns.

But by the 1980s the landmark
building had fallen into disrepair
and was threatened with demolition
– until a team of residents raised
the money to buy and restore it. In
1996 the theatre reopened its doors
(exterior renovations continued
into the 21st century). Today it is
one of the busiest cultural centres in
Hawaii, hosting hula performances,
comedy and film screenings. Say
hello to the diligent team of ushers
dressed in teal waistcoats with lei
around their necks; they are a wealth
of information on the theatre and
on Honolulu itself.
*1130 Bethel Street*
*+1 808 528 0506*
*hawaiitheatre.com*

*I'm just getting the lei of the land*

Doris Duke Theatre, Makiki
*Picture this*

The Honolulu Museum of Art
has been showing films since
the 1930s when screenings took
place in the central courtyard.
Today the museum has this
280-seat theatre; Honolulu's
only arthouse cinema and the
main venue for a brimming
programme of independent
and international films, plus
lectures and musical performances.

The theatre was named after
heiress and philanthropist Doris
Duke, whose foundation paid
for its refurbishment in 2000.
Duke's Diamond Head house,
Shangri-La, is also open to the
public (*see page 102*). The entrance
to the theatre is on Kinau Street
at the side of the museum and
tickets are available on the day
or online. Doors open half an
hour before the start.
*900 South Beretania Street*
*+1 808 532 6097*
*honolulumuseum.org*

### Screen fest

When it debuted in 1981 at the
University of Hawaii Manoa,
the Hawaii International Film
Festival showcased seven
films. Today it features about
150 from around the world.
The main festival takes place
in November, supported by
year-round screenings
and seminars.
*hiff.org*

③
Movie Museum, Kaimuki
*Picture box*

The Movie Museum might be the
only cinema in Hawaii showing
*Tiempo de Valientes*, *Mr Holmes* and
*Shaun the Sheep* in the same month.
This small set-up – just 19 leather
recliners on risers facing a 3.5 metre
by 2.5 metre screen – has been run by
Dwight Damon since 1991. Damon,
who previously led the Hawaii
International Film Festival's selection
committee, shows up to three films
a day. The venue also functions as
an archive and video-rental shop,
making 16,000 titles available on
VHS and about 6,000 on DVD.
We recommend reserving your
seats in advance.
*3566 Harding Avenue*
*+1 808 735 8771*

## Hawaii on screen

The lush islands have featured in dozens of films; here's a notable selection.

01 **From Here to Eternity (1953):** Fred Zinnemann's Oscar-winning adaptation of James Jones's 1951 novel is set in Hawaii in the run-up to Pearl Harbor and stars Burt Lancaster, Montgomery Clift, Deborah Kerr and Frank Sinatra. The famous scene with Lancaster and Kerr frolicking in the surf was shot at Halona Cove, east of Honolulu.

02 **Blue Hawaii (1961):** Featherlight comedy musical, the first of three films Elvis made in Hawaii (it was followed by *Girls! Girls! Girls!* and *Paradise, Hawaiian Style*). Locations included Waikiki Beach, Hanauma Bay and Diamond Head.

03 **Jurassic Park (1993):** Or, as it's also known, Kualoa Ranch. The 1,600-hectare site has been dubbed "Hawaii's back lot" and features in more than 50 Hollywood films and television shows including *Godzilla, Hawaii Five-0* and *Lost*. Open for pre-booked tours.

04 **The Descendants (2011):** George Clooney stars in this fine drama directed by Alexander Payne that delves into the lives of a distinct Hawaiian type: old-money Manoa *haoles* who frequent the Outrigger Canoe Club and send their children to Punahou School.

05 **Aloha (2015):** This Bradley Cooper vehicle is most memorable for a cameo by Hawaiian nationalist leader Dennis "Bumpy" Pu'uhonua Kanahele.

## Other
Creative enterprises

 The Arts at Marks Garage, Chinatown
*Drive-in culture*

This community arts centre is a key player in the drive to revitalise Chinatown; its schedule includes performance, talks and art shows. The building houses a good-looking multi-storey car park designed by Honolulu architect Ken Roehrig.
*1159 Nuuanu Avenue*
*+1 808 521 2903*
*artsatmarks.com*

**②**
Hawaii Symphony Orchestra, Downtown
*Classical virtues*

The Hawaii Symphony Orchestra was founded in 1900 as the Honolulu Symphony Orchestra; heavy debts forced it to disband in 2010 but it was revived with a new name the following year.

The orchestra appears regularly at the Neal S Blaisdell Concert Hall in Downtown, which also hosts sporting events and major stars (Elvis Presley filmed his famous *Aloha from Hawaii* concert here in 1973, see page 74). The musical programme is designed to appeal to a broad audience, with performances such as Byron Yasui's Concerto for Ukulele and Orchestra featuring ukulele superstar Jake Shimabukuro, and the accessible *Music that Pops* series featuring anything from 80s hits to a Judy Garland tribute.
*Neal S Blaisdell Center*
*777 Ward Avenue*
*+1 808 768 5400*
*hawaiisymphonyorchestra.org*

Play time
—
Explore this
multipurpose
indoor park

③
Kaka'ako Agora, Kaka'ako
*New sense of purpose*

This unique community space
is one of the latest additions to
the up-and-coming Kaka'ako
neighbourhood. By repurposing a
disused warehouse, Japanese firm
Atelier Bow-Wow has created an
airy "indoor park" with a spacious
mezzanine to hold a variety of
events in a shaded (and dry in
the rainy season) environment.

The space is run by Interisland
Terminal, a not-for-profit arts
collaborative that offers a diverse
programme of events, including art
exhibitions, film screenings, dance
workshops, Hawaiian storytelling
and taiko drumming.
*441 Cooke Street*
*kakaakoagora.org*

**Urasenke Tea House**

In a wooden two-storey
building amid Waikiki's
shops and hotel towers,
practitioners of Japan's
ancient tea ceremony host
weekly demonstrations for
visitors. This wood-and-tatami-
mat teahouse is run by the
Urasenke Foundation of
Hawaii, the local branch of
an organisation that traces
its origins to the 16th-century
tea master Sen Rikyu.
The ceremony isn't just
about sipping tea: it's
also about the pottery
and lacquerware, seasonal
sweets, ritualised gestures
and Japanese hospitality.
*urasenke.org*

## Bright stars

Since 1978, every spring Honolulu hosts Hawaii's best musical acts for the Na Hoku Hanohano Awards, the state's equivalent of the Grammy Awards. Several winners have gone on to find fame at the Grammys in Los Angeles.
*nahokuhanohano.org*

## The military

Hawaii has hosted US army, navy and airforce bases since 1898. Today it's a strategic outpost in the Pacific; with more than 51,000 personnel, the military is Hawaii's second-largest employer. Here are a few related sites worth seeing.

**01  Pearl Harbor monuments:**
The scene of Japan's 7 December 1941 surprise attack has four sites: the *USS Arizona* Memorial for the 1,177 crew who died; the *Battleship Missouri* Memorial, the last active US battleship; the *USS Bowfin* Submarine Museum & Park; and the Pacific Aviation Museum.
*pearlharborhistoricsites.org*

**02  Hawaii Army Museum:**
Built in the early 1900s to protect Honolulu Harbor from invasion, this reinforced-concrete structure tells the story of Hawaii's military history.
*hiarmymuseumsoc.org*

**03  National Memorial Cemetery of the Pacific:**
This cemetery is the final resting place of the US war fallen from the first and second world wars, South Korea, Vietnam and the 19th-century Boxer Rebellion in China. It opened in 1949.
*cem.va.gov*

## Music
Listen up

Jazz Minds, Ala Moana
*Dance party*

Opened in 2006, this unpretentious jazz lounge hosts Honolulu-based and out-of-town bands. It's not far from Waikiki in an area that was once seedy but has since perked up. You might even enjoy yourself enough to join the couples who often strut their stuff on the dance floor.
*1661 Kapi'olani Boulevard*
*+1 808 945 0800*
*honolulujazzclub.com*

Waikiki Shell, Waikiki
*Surround sound*

Opened in 1956, the 2,000-seat Waikiki Shell, tucked into the glorious Queen Kapi'olani Regional Park, is an iconic venue. Designed by Law & Wilson, its acoustics are much admired. The Beatles performed here in 1964 and a roster of musical heroes has since followed.
*2805 Monsarrat Avenue*
*+1 808 768 5400*
*blaisdellcenter.com*

## The Royal Hawaiian Band

The oldest and only full-time municipal band in the US, The Royal Hawaiian Band is one of Hawaii's most treasured cultural institutions. Established in 1836 by King Kamehameha III, the 40-piece band remains one of the islands' most effective ambassadors, travelling internationally and serenading visiting dignitaries with traditional and contemporary music. Some of the pieces in its repertoire were composed by Queen Lili'uokalani, Hawaii's last monarch, whose songs are among the most recognisable melodies on the islands today. The ensemble performs every Friday at midday at 'Iolani Palace (*see page 89*) and on Sundays at 14.00 at the bandstand in Queen Kapi'olani Regional Park, weather permitting.
*rhb-music.com*

## Nature
Flora and fauna

(1)
Lyon Arboretum, Upper Manoa
*Into the woods*

This lush 78-hectare arboretum and research centre, run by the University of Hawaii, sits at the top end of the Manoa Valley and is dedicated to preserving and studying the plant life of the islands. The arboretum dates back to 1919 when the Hawaiian Sugar Planters' Association, concerned by the effects of deforestation on the water supply, bought land in Manoa and asked Dr Harold Lyon, a plant pathologist, to test which trees would be suitable for reforestation.

Drive up past the entrance to the Manoa Falls trail and you will feel the air getting heavier. Pick up a trail map at the visitor centre and head out for a leisurely walk. There are species of native species, such as the iconic hula flower, the red-and-yellow *'ohi'a lehua*, and an ethnobotanical garden with plants used in Hawaiian culture. If you walk as far as 'Aihualama Falls it will take you about 40 minutes each way. Be warned though: the arboretum is in an area of damp tropical forest, which gets four metres of rain per year. Make use of insect repellent and wear some decent footwear since the paths can be slippery.
*3860 Manoa Road*
*+1 808 988 0456*
*manoa.hawaii.edu/lyonarboretum*

(2)
Waikiki Aquarium, Waikiki
Water world

The second-oldest public aquarium in the US, this marine-life mainstay was started in 1904 by the Honolulu Rapid Transit and Land Company to exhibit specimens from the reefs. Taking over in 1919, the University of Hawaii now uses it for research.
*2777 Kalakaua Avenue*
*+1 808 923 9741*
*waikikiaquarium.org*

### Three more gardens

**01** Foster Botanical Garden, Chinatown: Honolulu's oldest botanical garden is an unexpected find on the edge of Chinatown. Among its 5.5 hectares are trees planted in the 1850s by Dr William Hillebrand, a German botanist who lived on the site.
*+1 808 522 7060*

**02** Koko Crater Botanical Garden, Hawaii Kai: Plants occupy 24 hectares of the 81-hectare crater, set aside for a garden in 1958. The speciality here is endangered plants that flourish in lava fields and dryland forests, once widespread on the islands.
*+1 808 522 7060*

**03** Lili'uokalani Botanical Garden, Kuakini: The last monarch of Hawaii, Queen Lili'uokalani, donated this land to the city.
*+1 808 522 7060*

## Literature
Word of mouth

(1)
Mixing Innovative Arts, Chinatown
*Cocktail hour*

Launched in 2009, this monthly event and workshop series brings together some of Hawaii's most creative souls for a night of music, readings and spoken-word performances. It's a convivial affair: audiences mingle with the artists over a potent cocktail or two at Chinatown's The Manifest bar.
*32 North Hotel Street*
*miahonolulu.com*

Bamboo Ridge Press, citywide
*Independent state*

Founded by Eric Chock and Darrell Lum in 1978, publisher Bamboo Ridge Press is widely regarded as the primary source for new Hawaiian literature. It publishes two volumes a year: a poetry anthology alongside a work by a single author or an anthology on a special theme. Bamboo Ridge hosts seminars and workshops throughout the year.
*bambooridge.com*

③
University of Hawaii at Manoa,
Manoa
*Book club*

Hawaii's rich literary pedigree is
celebrated throughout the year at
the University of Hawaii at Manoa
through symposia, talks and lectures.
The Marjorie Putnam Sinclair Edel
Reading Series, named in honour
of the Hawaiian poet and novelist,
is a highlight: authors are invited to
read their work before an audience of
students, faculty and literary-minded
members of the public. The school
sponsors lectures on prominent
international authors, not least a
symposium on the Japanese writer
Haruki Murakami, that was attended
by the novelist himself.
*2500 Campus Road*
*manoa.hawaii.edu*

④
Friends of the Library of
Hawaii, Aiea
*Shelf lives*

If you're in Honolulu in mid-June,
be sure to meander among the trestle
tables laid out in the canteen of South
King Street's McKinley High School.
Stacked high with dog-eared books
donated from across the islands,
this annual book sale, approaching
its 70th anniversary, is the marquee
event of Friends of the Library of
Hawaii, an organisation founded
in 1879 to promote reading on the
islands. Today it works to support the
archipelago's 50 public libraries, and
hosts readings and smaller book sales
throughout the year.
*99-1132 Iwaena Street*
*+1 808 536 4174*
*friendsofthelibraryofhawaii.org*

**Top title**
—
The monthly *Honolulu Magazine*
traces its roots back to 1888
when King David Kalakaua
commissioned it in order to
promote the state globally.
Called *Paradise of the Pacific*, it
became *Honolulu Magazine* in
1966 and switched its focus to
news, features and profiles for
local readers.

**Best of the rest**
Media round-up

① 
Print
*Reading material*

The print-media outlets here
neatly capture Hawaii's distinctive
atmosphere. You'll find the
resurgent urban scene reflected
in the pages of ❶ *Foundry*. The
islands' many surfers get their own
magazine ❷ *Freesurf*, while the
handsome lifestyle magazine
❸ *Flux* offers insight into art and
culture. ❹ *Contrast*, founded by
graphic designer and photographer
Mark Kushimi, takes a fresh look
at art, music and design. ❺ *Edible*
is a quarterly that celebrates the
state's culinary richness. For news
the city's daily ❻ *Honolulu Star-
Advertiser* is a popular choice that
was first published in 2010 when
two venerable papers were brought
together: the 128-year-old *Honolulu
Star-Bulletin* and the 154-year-old
*Honolulu Advertiser*. ❼ *Trim* is a
stylish bilingual (Japanese-English)
guide to surf culture; and for the
discerning traveller we recommend
Mokulele Airline's superior in-flight
journal ❽ *Hopper*.

**Radio**

Hawaii's first commercial radio
aired in 1922 and the state now
has 60 stations specialising
in music, religion and current
affairs, broadcasting in English,
Japanese and Korean.

**01** Hawaii Public Radio:
HPR broadcasts news,
talkshows, music and a
programme on astronomy.
*hpr2.org*

**02** Kine105FM: A standard-
bearer of Hawaiian music,
Kine plays Kuana Torres
Kahele, Cyril Pahinui,
Chad Takatsugi, Blayne
Asing and more.
*hawaiian105.com*

**03** Aloha Broha: DJ Joncozy,
rapper Kwalified and
musician Science Ben
delve into Hawaii's
cultural life.
*alohabroha.com*

# Design and architecture
—— Hidden gems

Honolulu doesn't get much credit for its design pedigree but anyone interested in modernism will love its retro offices, homes, shops and hotels. Bleached by the sun and built with a modish mix of concrete, steel and native materials such as koa wood, these structures from the 1950s to 1970s are at home in the heat and humidity.

Tropical modernism – a style perfected by Vladimir Ossipoff – is everywhere. Look out for terrific bank buildings, government offices, churches and some stellar signage, relics of the days when Honolulu was being transformed from a rural economy into a modern centre. If you're after something older, head to 'Iolani Palace, Chinatown or the early buildings around Merchant Street. Recent years have seen a flurry of skyscrapers being built, with mixed results. The non-profit organisation Historic Hawaii Foundation (*historichawaii.org*) preserves Honolulu's architectural heritage, which is frequently under threat from developers.

**Vladimir Ossipoff**
Tropical modernist

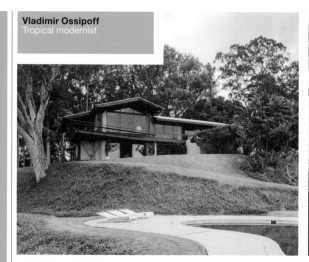

Ideal home
——
Ossipoff's design is open and spacious

IBM Building, Kaka'ako
*Under the sun*

Ossipoff was adept at combining the latest steel and concrete construction techniques with façades adapted to local conditions. The 1962 IBM Building set back from Ala Moana Boulevard is a seven-storey concrete structure with glass windows hidden beneath a 1,360-piece geometric concrete grille. The grille shades the interior but with its Polynesian design also roots the building in its tropical location, or, as Ossipoff put it, "gives the building a sense of belonging in the sun". The architect called it his favourite office. At one time the building was threatened with demolition; it is now part of Ward Village, a 24-hectare development.
*1240 Ala Moana Boulevard*

## Vladimir Ossipoff

Hawaiian modernism deserves greater recognition, not least for its finest exponent Vladimir Ossipoff (1907 to 1998). Vladivostok-born Ossipoff spent his childhood in Japan and graduated from the University of California, Berkeley in 1931. He then moved to Honolulu where, over the course of a 67-year career, he forged a distinctive style – parts Japanese, Hawaiian and international modernist – that was well suited to the tropical climate. Although Ossipoff's remaining homes are highly prized today, many of his works have not survived and modernist buildings are rarely safe from developers.
*historichawaii.org*

① Liljestrand House,
Tantalus-Makiki Heights
*Finest hour*

This hillside residence on Mount Tantalus was completed in 1952 for Betty and Howard Liljestrand. They were demanding clients but the result was architect Vladimir Ossipoff's finest hour: a handsome residence with views from every room. Many of the materials, such as the Big Island ohia hardwood, were sourced locally. Japanese craftsmen were responsible for the interior carpentry, which is, like the rest of the house, pristine. Betty and Howard's son Bob still lives on the property and visitors can see the house on small group tours.
*3300 Tantalus Drive*
*+1 808 537 3116*
*liljestrandhouse.org*

### Ossipoff's works

**01** Honolulu International Airport
*hawaii.gov/hnl*
**02** Outrigger Canoe Club
*outriggercanoeclub.com*
**03** Ossipoff Archive at The Hamilton Library at the University of Hawaii at Manoa
*library.manoa.hawaii.edu*

③
Robert Shipman Thurston Jr
Memorial Chapel, Manoa
*Ancient and modern*

Ossipoff designed several buildings
at Punahou School in Manoa. This
chapel, dedicated in 1967, was the gift
of Mr and Mrs Robert S Thurston,
whose son was killed in the Second
World War. It sits at the school's lily
pond (part of which is incorporated
into the chapel) and its freshwater
spring, Ka Punahou. With its
distinctive copper-and-clay roof and
koa-wood pews sloping down to a
coral altar, the chapel is both modern
and Hawaiian. Look out for the
stained-glass windows by the artist
Erica Karawina, whose works appear
in many buildings around Honolulu.
*1601 Punahou Street*
*punahou.edu*

④
University of Hawaii Administration
Building (Bachman Hall), Manoa
*Smart building*

Local materials added to the island
flavour of this administration
building from 1949: coral lends
texture and a light pink colour to
the concrete walkways and courtyard,
while the boardroom walls are in
koa wood. Carefully angled concrete
columns shield the sun.
*2444 Dole Street*
*manoa.hawaii.edu*

**Places of worship**
Spiritual spaces

①
Liliha Shingonji Mission, Liliha
*Traditional values*

Many pass this temple without
noticing it but it's the oldest in
Oʻahu. Built in 1911, it incorporates a
more traditional style of architecture.
In keeping with Shingon temples
in Japan the sanctuary is filled with
objects, such as lanterns and images
of the sect's founder Kobo Daishi.
*1710 Liliha Street*
*+1 808 533 3929*
*koyasanshingonhawaii.org*

*If you need any new deities, let me know*

**Buddhist temples**

Japanese immigrants brought
Buddhism with them and built
temples in a range of styles,
including one unique to Hawaii,
known as Indian-Western. It
is thought there were once
more than 300 temples but
with a decline in the Buddhist
population, some have fallen
into disrepair. Others are faring
better and are the place to go
during the Bon dancing season
from June to mid-September.

**01** Jodo Mission of Hawaii,
Lower Makiki: Built in
1932, this pink temple is
regularly mistaken for a
mosque; it is in fact the
most famous example of
the Indian-Western style.
*jodo.us*

**02** Honolulu Myohoji
Mission, Nuʻuanu:
Myohoji is a hidden oasis.
Its main hall and pagoda,
designed by Hawaiian-
born architect Robert
Katsuyoshi, were
dedicated in 1968. The
temple holds Japanese
culture classes and
meditation sessions
every Friday from 18.00.
*honolulumyohoji.org*

Divine details
—
Preis's build mixes concrete and lava rock

Modernist churches
—
01 Community Church of Honolulu
*cchonolulu.org*
02 St Augustine by the Sea
*staugustinebythesea.com*
03 Calvary by the Sea
*calvarybythesea.org*

**②**
First United Methodist Church, Makiki
*Intelligent design*

In the 1950s and 1960s, modernism started appearing in Honolulu's houses of worship. In his celebrated Methodist church on South Beretania Street, completed in 1953, Austrian-born architect Alfred Preis used lava rock, a concrete altar and sliding windows that brought the outside in.

Preis was a key figure in Honolulu architecture, not only for his still-sought-after mid-century residences: as state planning co-ordinator he worked on the overall design of the Capitol district.
*1020 South Beretania Street*
*+1 808 522 9565*
*firstumchonolulu.org*

**State buildings**
By official approval

①
Hawaii State Capitol, Downtown
*State of grace*

Honolulu struck the jackpot with its State Capitol, built a decade after Hawaii became the 50th state in the US in 1959. Designed by John Carl Warnecke with Belt, Lemmon & Lo, it combines the heft of government with Hawaiian informality, using local motifs and materials, such as the volcanic stone that clads the cone structure housing the two soaring legislative chambers.

Look out for details such as the nautilus shell chandelier (representing the moon) in the Senate and its gold-plated counterpart (the sun) in the House of Representatives, both by German artist Otto Piene.

It's open to the public on weekdays year-round, 08.30 to 15.30. Guided tours are given at 13.00 on Wednesdays from January to May and on Mondays and Wednesdays from June to December.
*415 South Beretania Street*
*+1 808 974 4000*
*governor.hawaii.gov/hawaii-state-capitol-tours*

② Walter Murray Gibson Building,
Downtown
*Arresting style*

This four-storey Mediterranean-
looking building, completed in 1931,
served as Honolulu Police Station
until 1967. After that it was a district
court building and still houses
city offices today. It was designed
by Louis Davis, a US architect
renowned for making buildings in the
Spanish colonial and mission revival
style. Davis was responsible for some
of Honolulu's classic (now sadly
defunct) cinemas.

For the police station he
used terracotta portals, mahogany
doors and 11 tonnes of Rojo
Alicante marble.
*842 Bethel Street (corner of
Merchant Street)*

**Three more Merchant Street
Historic District structures**

01 **Melchers Building:**
Honolulu's oldest
commercial building was
constructed in 1854 using
coral stone.
*51 Merchant Street*
02 **Yokohama Specie Bank:**
This was designed for the
Japanese bank in 1909
by Honolulu architect
Henry Livingston Kerr.
*36 Merchant Street*
03 **Royal Saloon:** This
watering hole was built
in 1890 for wealthy
landowner Walter
Chamberlain "WC"
Peacock, who went on to
build the historic Moana
Hotel in Waikiki (today
known as the Moana
Surfrider, see page 24).
*2 Merchant Street*

③
Jefferson Hall, East-West
Center, Manoa
*Global vision*

Chinese-American architect IM
Pei went on to great fame with
his Louvre Pyramid but his early
Honolulu work includes this compact
but monumental 1963 building for
the East-West Center, an organisation
established in 1960 to promote good
relations between Asia, the Pacific
and the US.

The Center occupies 8.5 hectares
on the University of Hawaii's Manoa
campus. The tranquil Japanese
garden, completed in the same year,
was designed by landscape architect
Kenzo Ogata and blessed in 1964
by then Crown Prince Akihito and
Crown Princess Michiko. If you peek
inside Pei's building, look out for the
futuristic stairwell murals by David
Barker, an art student back in 1967.
Pei designed several buildings for
the Center, including the Kennedy
Theater across the road.
*1601 East-West Road
+1 808 944 7111
eastwestcenter.org*

Hawaii State Public Library,
Downtown
*By the book*

O'ahu's library was funded by
philanthropist Andrew Carnegie
and designed by his brother-in-law
Henry D Whitfield. It was completed
in 1913 but remodelled in 1929 by
Charles William Dickey to make it
look more Hawaiian, with a leafy
courtyard and *lanai* (veranda) on the
upper floor that remain popular spots
for readers. It received another, less
extensive update in 1992.
    Hawaii has an impressive
statewide library system: non-
residents can become temporary
members for a small fee.
*478 South King Street*
*+1 808 586 3500*
*hawaii.sdp.sirsi.net*

Ⓢ
Department of Transportation
Building, Downtown
*Upwardly mobile*

This five-storey structure known
as Ali'i'aimoku Hale occupies a
prominent spot on Punchbowl
Street and boasts striking vertical
sun shields. It was built for the
Territorial Department of Highways
in 1959 and designed by Law &
Wilson. Robert Law came to Hawaii
during his spell in the US navy and
stayed on after the war, while James
B Wilson was born in Hawaii. They
started their firm in 1947 and works
include the 1956-built Waikiki Shell
(*see page 93*) and the Church of the
Holy Nativity (1954).
*869 Punchbowl Street*
*+1 808 587 2150*
*hidot.hawaii.gov*

**Living spaces**
Residential highlights

Ⓘ
Queen Emma Gardens, Downtown
*East meets West*

Japanese-American architect Minoru
Yamasaki may be best known for his
1973 World Trade Center in New
York but this apartment development
became a Honolulu landmark when it
was completed in 1963.
    The three residential blocks –
called King, Queen and Prince – sit
in three well-manicured hectares; its
two main towers, both 23 storeys,
are visible from across the city.
Yamasaki combined East and
West here: shoji screens and *lanai*
(verandas) in the apartments;
swimming pools, a jogging path,
koi ponds and Japanese teahouses
in the garden.
*1511-1519 Nu'uanu Avenue*
*queenemma.com*

Ⓩ
Ward Village, Kaka'ako
*Regeneration game*

This ongoing project is urban
transformation on a grand scale:
24.2 hectares of coastal property
in the middle of the city is being
developed by the American company
Howard Hughes Corporation into a
new urban village. The masterplan
includes three soaring residential
towers, a 1.6-hectare park, two
more luxury towers designed by
Richard Meier overlooking Kewalo
Basin Harbour and shopping
neighbourhoods that also offer
places to eat and a 16-screen
multiplex. The 424-unit Ke
Kilohana block is reserved for
first-time buyers resident in Hawaii
and was sold by public lottery.
*wardvillage.com*

Ⓣ
Shangri-La Center for Islamic
Arts and Cultures, Kahala
*Taste for the exotic*

American heiress Doris Duke visited
Hawaii as part of her lavish around-
the-world honeymoon in 1935. She
fell in love with the place and bought
two hectares of land at Ka'alawai
Beach. Today visitors can see Duke's
stunning estate on guided tours.
    The house is a vivid marriage of
the owner's exuberant taste and her
collection of Islamic art, which she
continued to build until her death
in 1993. Tiled murals from Isfahan,
Moroccan wooden ceilings and
painted Syrian interiors can all be
found here. Book well in advance.
*4055 Papu Circle*
*+1 808 734 1941*
*shangrilahawaii.org*

**Traditional structures**
Out of the past

① Kawaiahaʻo Church, Downtown
*Rock of ages*

This grand-looking church next to a group of mission houses (*see page 104*) was dedicated in 1842 but its roots go back two decades beforehand to when the first missionaries arrived from the mainland. They were granted land here – the site of a freshwater spring – by King Kamehameha III, who called for the construction of a stone church. The resulting place of worship took 14,000 slabs of coral to build. The cemetery is well worth a look too. This is one the few churches to offer services in Hawaiian.
*957 Punchbowl Street*
*+1 808 469 3000*
*kawaiahao.org*

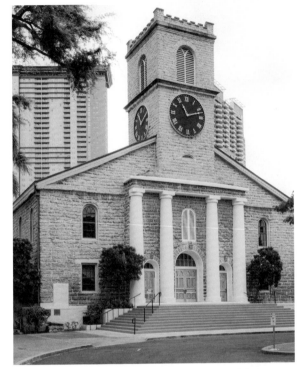

**2**

Hawaiian mission houses, Downtown
*Back in time*

These three restored houses –
two of them the oldest in Hawaii
– were the homes and workplaces
of Hawaii's first missionaries. They
were led by the redoubtable Hiram
Bingham, the Vermont-born settler
who first landed in Hawaii in 1820.
The oldest mission house was
shipped from Boston in the same
year as Bingham's arrival and built
in 1821. The other two were built in
1831 and 1841 using coral blocks
cut from the reef.

All three are open for guided
tours, which take place from
Tuesday to Saturday on the
hour from 11.00 to 15.00. For
anyone interested in the history
of Honolulu and the Hawaiian
language there is a well-stocked
bookshop. The Mission Social
Hall and Café (*see page 33*), run by
chef Mark Noguchi, is a popular
lunch spot.
*553 South King Street*
*+ 1 808 447 3910*
*missionhouses.org*

*Living history*
—
This Hawaii
landmark
was built in
1821

**Commercial buildings**
All business

**1**

Occidental Life Insurance
Building, Makiki
*Ground control*

Residents of Honolulu seem to
have mixed feelings about this
concrete, sandstone and glass
building, designed by prolific firm
Lemmon & Freeth back in 1951
for Occidental's Hawaii outpost.
The cantilevered tower, which
has more than a hint of an airport
control tower, and an extra floor
were added in 1967 and give the
otherwise unspectacular building its
modernist feel. The company name
has been Occidental Underwriters
of Hawaii since 1954 but for many
the old name still stands.
*1163 South Beretania Street*
*+ 1 808 536 1933*
*askoxy.com*

**2**

Aloha Tower, Downtown
*High society*

The Aloha Tower opened in 1926
and was once the tallest building
in Hawaii. Topped by the word
"Aloha", the harbour lighthouse
offered a warm welcome to tourists
and immigrants. The arrival of a
big ship was dubbed Boat Day
and the city put on a festive show,
greetings passengers with music
and hula dancing. Recent attempts
to develop the area around the
tower as a shopping centre have
been less than successful and these
days the famous landmark is best
appreciated from a distance. It
is open to visitors from 09.30 to
sunset and admission is free.
*155 Ala Moana Boulevard*
*alohatower.com*

**Charles William Dickey**
Pop's art

①
Honolulu Hale, Downtown
*Twenties vision*

It took some time after annexation by the US in 1898 for Hawaii to find its feet architecturally but its identity as the cultural crossroads of the Pacific had come into sharper focus by the 1920s. Classical conventions gave way to a Mediterranean – and more Hawaiian – style, as demonstrated by Honolulu Hale, the city's official seat of government. Part designed by Charles William Dickey and Hart

Wood and completed in 1929, it mixes Spanish Revival and Italianate styles. There's an interior courtyard and tiled floor and roof.
*530 South King Street*
*+1 808 768 6622*
*honolulu.gov*

Alexander & Baldwin Building, Downtown
*Sweet retreat*

Designed by Charles William Dickey and Hart Wood, this striking building from 1929 was named after Samuel Thomas Alexander and Henry Perrine Baldwin, founders of a powerful Hawaiian sugar company.

There was nothing fancy about the materials – steel and concrete – but details such as the double-pitch tiled roof and top-floor balcony make it a memorable landmark. Wood, who came to Hawaii in 1919, was overshadowed by his illustrious partner but he is admired for his East-meets-West Hawaiian regionalist style. This was their last building together.
*822 Bishop Street*

**Charles William Dickey**

Dickey (1871-1942), known to his peers as "Pop", was the foremost architect in Hawaii during the late 1920s and 1930s. He grew up on Maui, was educated on the mainland and spent 20 years in California before returning to Honolulu. His work incorporates Californian mission and Chinese and Japanese elements but he made his name with his unique Hawaiian style: open villas with double-pitched hip roofs and wide eaves that suited the tropical climate.

**01** Stangenwald Building, 1901: This Italianate-style office building was hailed as Honolulu's first high-rise.
*119 Merchant Street*

**02** Central Fire Station, 1934: This art deco beauty replaced the old lava-rock Central Station from 1897.
*104 South Beretania Street*

**03** US Immigration Building, 1934: This building has the Dickey touch: wide eaves, a pitched roof and Chinese accents.
*595 Ala Moana Boulevard*

**Signs**
Just our type

01  02

03  04

05  06

07

08

09   10

11

## Sign of the times

They adorn the sides of hotels, apartment blocks and low-rise office buildings: decades-old signs discoloured by years of exposure to rain, wind and sun. Though their stories are often long forgotten, these relics are as much a part of the urban landscape as lava-rock walls and breezeblocks.

We asked Hawaii-based graphic artist Matthew Tapia, who creates logos, typefaces and signs for a living, to identify a few favourites from among Honolulu's distinctive signs.

**01** Hawaiian King (1959), Waikiki:
*417 Nohonani Street*

**02** King Center (1960), Ala Moana:
*1451 South King Street*

**03** Royal Grove Hotel (1962), Waikiki:
*151 Uluniu Avenue*

**04** Kaiulani Kai Apartment (circa 1960), Waikiki:
*239 Kaiulani Avenue*

**05** The Breakers (1954), Waikiki:
*250 Beach Walk*

**06** Waikiki Grand Hotel, (1962), Waikiki:
*134 Kapahulu Avenue*

**07** The Leiahua (1965), Waikiki:
*1993 Ala Wai Boulevard*

**08** Royal Hawaiian Hotel (1927), Waikiki:
*2259 Kalakaua Avenue*

**09** The Honolulu Brewing and Malt Company (1900), Kaka'ako:
*533 Queen Street*

**10** Like Like Drive Inn (1953), Ala Moana:
*745 Keeaumoku Street*

**11** Waikiki Skyliner (1966), Waikiki:
*2415 Ala Wai Boulevard*

King of the surf — Fans pay their respects to Duke with lei

(1)
Duke Kahanamoku statue, Waikiki
*Chairman of the board*

On 27 January 1968, Honolulu was a city in mourning: Duke Kahanamoku was dead. Flags flew at half mast and thousands gathered to bid farewell to the father of modern surfing. The Waikiki beachboys sang traditional songs as a flotilla of canoes and mourners on surfboards escorted his ashes out to sea.

In 1990, sculptor Jan Gordon Fisher's statue of Duke, a three-time Olympic swimming champion, was unveiled: a larger-than-life bronze artwork backed by a longboard, arms outstretched to his devotees. Duke served as sheriff of Honolulu and became one of the city's first official greeters in his final years.
*Kalakaua Avenue*

(2)
Natatorium War Memorial, Waikiki
*Monument to neglect*

Opened in 1927, this saltwater swimming pool was a monument to the servicepeople who died in

the First World War. After it was turned over to the city in 1949 the monument was neglected and today survives in decayed splendour.
*2815 Kalakaua Avenue*
*+808 254 1828*
*natatorium.org*

(3)
USS Arizona Memorial, Pearl Harbor
*Troubled water*

An Elvis concert in O'ahu helped make up the shortfall in funds for this Alfred Preis-designed 1962 memorial to the servicemen who died in the Japanese attack on Pearl Harbor. It is an unusual proposition: a low-slung bridge spanning the still-visible sunken battleship, the *USS Arizona*, which is the resting place for most of the 1,177 lost crew. The memorial is Hawaii's top attraction, with 1.8 million visitors a year taken out on shuttle boats. Book ahead or come early (from 07.00) for one of the 2,000 tickets handed out daily on a first come, first served basis.
*1 Arizona Memorial Place*
*+1 808 422 3399*
*pearlharborhistoricsites.org*

(1)
Love's Bakery, citywide
*Fresh prints*

The logo is a familiar sight to Hawaiians: slanted black letters with a heart where an apostrophe would be, set against a yellow background. It's on the bags of 230,000kg of bread, doughnuts and cakes made weekly at the company's Honolulu factory and sold to grocery stores, restaurants, schools, hospitals and military bases on five of Hawaii's islands.

Founded in 1851 by Robert Love, a Scot, the locally owned company is the largest wholesale baker in the state. The logo tells Hawaiians that they're getting fresh bread, not loaves that have been frozen and sent from the mainland.
*lovesbakeryhawaii.com*

(2)
Bike racks, citywide
*Revolutionary cycle*

In the 1990s, then-mayor Jeremy Harris was tasked with improving the city's cycling infrastructure. Motivating residents to ditch their cars and use their bikes was a challenge. The mayor believed that novel, well-designed racks would give cyclists somewhere to lock up their wheels and also serve as a subtle visual reminder of cycling as a mode of transport around the city.

So Honolulu's first bicycle-shaped bike racks – made in Minneapolis – were installed. They can hold up to four bikes at a time and the handlebars of each one are placed in the direction of travel on its given side of the road to help orientate cyclists when they get back in the saddle.

(3)
Pavement language lessons, Waikiki
*Word on the street*

If you find yourself on Kalakaua Avenue, look down. Engraved into the pavement will be a common Hawaiian word with its English translation beneath. These fragments of Hawaii's native vocabulary were introduced by the city council in 2011 as part of the refurbishment of Waikiki's public spaces, an initiative that began in the mid-1980s.

# Sport and fitness
—— Get moving

With its tropical climate and long coastline, Honolulu is an outdoor-enthusiast's paradise. Thanks to warm ocean temperatures year-round, there's no shortage of water sports: surfing, outrigger canoeing, stand-up paddle-boarding, ocean swimming and sea kayaking. If you prefer firm ground we have recommendations for trails to hike, city footpaths to run and roads to cycle.

But don't limit yourself to these: it's just as easy to hop in a car and find an isolated beach or trail that suits you. And when you've finished your workout and want to look and feel your best, we have suggestions for spas and shaves.

**Watersports**
Liquid assets

**Surf school**
Waikiki's beachboys are top teachers

**①**
Surfing, Waikiki
*Learn from the best*

Since the early 1900s, many Hawaiian surfers have made a living teaching tourists how to ride the gentle waves of Waikiki. These so-called "beachboys" are famous – and popular with visitors – for their carefree lifestyle, easygoing demeanour and in-depth knowledge of swells. Over the years they have introduced everyone from royalty and movie stars to average joes to the joys of surfing.

While there are more than a few groups peddling lessons on the strip, the crew from Waikiki Beach Services, based out of the Royal Hawaiian Hotel, are among the most skilled and enthusiastic. Not only will you be learning from the best, but you'll be taking part in an age-old tradition with the people who taught the world to surf.
*2259 Kalakaua Avenue*
*+1 808 388 1510*
*waikikibeachservices.com*

(2)

Waikiki Swim Club, Waikiki
*Take a dip*

Swimming in the sea is one of the great pleasures of a trip to Honolulu. Waikiki Swim Club was founded in 1971 with the aim of promoting safe ocean swimming. Its website lists up-to-date information about tides, jellyfish, safe practice (such as wearing a brightly coloured cap for visibility) and weekend group swims. The club also sponsors events on O'ahu, including the North Shore Swim Series and the 2km Fin Swim at Ala Moana Beach Park. It also hosts biannual swimming clinics with the University of Hawaii Swim Team, which non-members can join.
*waikikiswimclub.org*

(3)

Palolo Valley District Park Pool, Palolo
*Go public*

It's hard to beat swimming in the ocean but if you're looking to do laps, head to this 50-metre outdoor pool in Palolo Valley District Park. It's free to use and open seven days a week. Check for opening times and lap-swimming hours.
*2007 Palolo Avenue*
*+1 808 733 7362*
*honolulu.gov*

**Good news: it's time to swap**

**Wave watching**
—
Before heading to the beach, check out surf conditions on O'ahu's webcams. California-based company Surfline also provides surf reports alongside weather and tide forecasts.
*livesurfcamhawaii.com; surfline.com*

## Surf spots

**01 Queens, Waikiki:** In the pantheon of surf breaks in Honolulu you'd be hard-pressed to find a wave more accommodating and steeped in history than this one. Located almost directly out to sea from the famous bronze statue of Duke Kahanamoku (*see page 108*), who often surfed here, Queens has been a haunt of countless generations of surfers. It's easy to see why: the wave is gentle enough for novices to find their footing but offers plenty of open face for more experienced surfers.

**02 Diamond Head:** At the base of the Diamond Head crater you'll find a well-established trail that snakes down the cliff and onto the beach. Unlike Waikiki, Diamond Head is open to prevailing trade winds that often blow out the surf but if you can stomach the chop and spray you'll find something to ride here nearly all yearround. Breaking over reef, this wave typically holds a bit more power than some other line-ups in Waikiki, making it better for those with more experience.

**03 Tonggs, near Diamond Head:** You'll find lovely left-breaking waves off a quaint neighbourhood between Waikiki and Diamond Head. There's no beach but Tonggs is great if you want a mellow session without crowds. To access the break, paddle about 140 metres out from the stairway off Kalakaua Avenue. The inside whitewater waves are best for beginners, while savvier surfers will find a forgiving left on the outside reef.

Tranquil waters
—
Currents are calmer in the summer months

④
Kayak to the Mokulua Islands, Kailua
*Grab a paddle*

The picturesque beachside community of Lanikai, just beyond Kailua, is a 800-metre strip of serene shoreline. Look out to sea and roughly 1.2km away you'll spot two islets: the Mokulua Islands (commonly referred to as "the Moks"). It's possible to reach them by kayak and such a jaunt is an ideal way to spend half a day.

While your muscles will be complaining from the arduous paddle, it's worth the sweat. Free from development and brimming with sea life, the Mokuluas are a must-see. You can rent your own kayak but we recommend scheduling a tour with the team at Twogood Kayaks, who know the area better than anyone.
*134B Hamakua Drive*
*+1 808 262 5656*
*twogoodkayaks.com*

### Bird's-eye view
To view O'ahu from a different angle, why not take a helicopter tour? Seeing the mountain ranges and sweeping beaches from the sky is a spectacular experience. Blue Hawaiian offers 45-minute tours every day.
*bluehawaiian.com*

⑤
Stand-up paddle to Kailua
*All stood up*

Over the past decade, stand-up paddling has exploded in popularity in coastal communities worldwide – and for good reason. It's fun, great exercise and offers a perspective of the ocean and other surroundings like no other. Consider heading east away from Waikiki and over Pali mountain to Kailua Town. From this quaint beachside community – where Barack Obama likes to spend his Christmas holidays – you'll find many surf shops and guides offering stand-up paddle tours. We suggest the team at Kailua Beach Adventures.
*130 Kailua Road*
*+1 808 262 2555*
*kailuasailboards.com*

## More water activities

**01** Shark tour, North Shore:
For a heart-thumping
experience, head to
Hale'iwa for a dip in
shark-infested waters.
North Shore Shark
Adventures has been
leading intrepid tourists
on these nail-biting tours
since 2001. From the
security of a cage
you will develop an
appreciation for these
graceful predators as
they glide past.
*sharktourshawaii.com*

**02** Hawaiian sailing canoe,
various locations: The
crew from Hawaiian Ocean
Adventures whisk visitors
around the Pacific in
hand-built sailing canoes
– vessels Polynesians
have used for millennia.
The tours involve parties
of no more than eight
meandering down the
west or east coast as
a guide explains the
land, people and history
of old Hawaii.
*hawaiianocean
adventures.com*

**03** Fireworks cruise, Waikiki:
It's not exactly a sport
but it's still an entertaining
way to spend time on the
water. Every Friday at
19.45 the Waikiki skyline
explodes with colour
thanks to a fireworks
show. While many choose
to watch from the beach,
the best vantage point is
from a boat anchored
just beyond the reef at
Waikiki. Hawaii Glass
Bottom Boats offers tours
that depart Kewalo Harbor
at 19.00.
*hawaiiglassbottomboats.com*

**⑥**
Snorkelling to Shark's Cove
*Underwater exploration*

Hawaii is home to many reef fish not
found anywhere else on Earth. When
the waves are calm, head to Shark's
Cove in Pupukea on the North
Shore or Hanauma Bay (*see page
114*). Look out for endemic species
such as masked angelfish, Hawaiian
cleaner wrasse and bluestripe
butterflyfish, as well as rays, eels,
green sea turtles and dolphins.
*Kamehameha Highway*

**⑦**
Outrigger canoes, Waikiki
*Oarsome activity*

If surfing the hallowed waves
of Waikiki isn't on your must-do
list, we recommend the next-best
thing: an outrigger canoe ride
through the line-up. It's a tad
touristy but exhilarating. Guided
by a trusty Waikiki beachboy,
your outrigger will navigate out
past the waders and surfers in
order to catch waves back in to
shore. There are a number of
different operations offering
canoe rides in the area but
Waikiki Beach Services (*see
page 110*) are our favourites
for this trip.
*2259 Kalakaua Avenue
+1 808 388 1510
waikikibeachservices.com*

## Best beaches
### Paradise found

**①**

Hanauma Bay, Hawaii Kai
*Wildlife wander*

As you drive east from Waikiki
the landscape dramatically shifts.
Travelling along Kalanianaole
Highway, dense urban surroundings
give way to stunning cliffs that
seem to rise straight from the sea
as you near Hanauma Bay State
Park. This protected bay does get
crowded but with good reason: its
nature preserve is one of the best
places in Hawaii to observe sealife.
Snorkelling in this scenic place is
a must; with any luck you'll spot
plenty of turtles.

**②**

Sunset Beach, Pupukea
*Winter waves*

In winter the North Shore is
thumped with some of the most
powerful – and infamous – surf
on the planet. Wave-riders flock
to Sunset Beach to test their
mettle on iconic breaks such as
Banzai Pipeline, Backdoor and
Off the Wall. The swells make it too
dangerous for swimming but come
summer the beach clears out and the
water becomes safe and inviting.

**③**

Kawela Bay, Koʻolauloa
*Laidback gem*

On the North Shore of Oʻahu,
just west of Turtle Bay Resort,
you'll find Kawela Bay. It's an
open and quiet tree-lined stretch
of beach that harks back to the
days before Hawaii became such a
tourist hotspot. Head here to
watch the sun go down, snorkel,
paddle-board or simply enjoy
doing nothing at all.

**④**

Kaimana Beach, Waikiki
*Popular choice*

Kaimana, at the southern reach of
Waikiki, is a busy place: you'll find
a mix of young families, children
learning to swim and groups
barbecuing on the park lawn.
It's also the site of the Natatorium
War Memorial (*see page 108*),
built in 1927 as a monument to
the Hawaiians who died in the
First World War.
  When facing the mountains
from the beach you won't see any
of the high-rise hotels but rather
the scenic expanse of Queen
Kapiʻolani Park. The beach itself
is relatively small but its waters are
protected from large south swells
by a barrier reef, so it's perfect for
wading and swimming.

**Name check**
—
Kaimana is also known as Sans Souci Beach

(5)
Lanikai Beach, Kailua
*Soothing sands*

Lanikai Beach lies on the eastern side of the island near the town of Kailua. Its length (almost a kilometre), turquoise waters and golden sands make it a popular option. Accessing it can be a headache if you've travelled by car but any frustration is quickly forgotten once you hit the postcard-perfect water to swim, kayak or paddle-board.

**Beach care**
—
Hawaii law considers shorelines to be public and a place of shared responsibility. Volunteer clean-ups are frequent and since sunscreen with oxybenzone is believed to contribute to coral bleaching, brands with zinc oxide as their active ingredient are encouraged.

## Lawn bowls
Gentle activity

*Bowled moves*
—
Shoes are optional for players

①
### Honolulu Lawn Bowls Club, Ala Moana
*Green and pleasant*

This lawn-bowls club was established in the mid-1930s for Australian troops stationed in Honolulu and is the only one in Hawaii. The rules are simple: players take turns to roll a bowl at a target and the one that ends up the closest wins.

The club welcomes visitors and every Saturday morning beginners can take free lessons; opening times do vary though so call ahead. Observe the etiquette: before and after matches, shake hands and say, "Good bowls". Distracting your opponent is frowned upon.
*Ala Moana Park*
*+1 808 388 0428*
*honolululawnbowls.com*

## Grooming
Prime preening

①
### Citizen Salon, Downtown
*Cutting edge*

A scalp massage and hot towel are a standard part of the grooming at owner-stylist Jaime Malapit's salon. Malapit, a graduate of the Vidal Sassoon Academy in California, leads a small team of talented stylists at his bright and airy shop. His clientele go as much for the exceptional hospitality as they do for the expert haircuts, colouring and treatments.
*12 South King Street*
*+1 808 533 3200*
*citizen-salon.com*

**②**
Mojo Barbershop & Social Club,
McCully-Moʻiliʻili
*The works*

Mojo is the quintessential
neighbourhood barbershop – with
added extras. It's the sort of place
where you can get a haircut and
straight-razor wet shave but also
a detox face treatment and beard
trim. Co-owners Marian Lee and
Matt Leo opened their first salon
in Chinatown in 2011 and have
now added this second shop on
South King Street. The salons
stock a variety of men's speciality
grooming products, from shaving
kits by Baxter of California to
Grant's Golden Brand Pomade.
*2005 South King Street*
*+1 808 800 3960*
*mojobarbershop.com*

**③**
Abhasa Waikiki Spa, Waikiki
*Serene sanctuary*

This spa in The Royal Hawaiian
hotel offers peace in the middle
of Waikiki. The Abhasa Harmony
massage combines traditional
Hawaiian *lomi lomi* technique with
Japanese shiatsu, while the After Sun
Skin Drench treatment is for anyone
who's overdone the sunshine.
*2259 Kalakaua Avenue*
*+1 808 922 8200*
*en.abhasa.com*

**④**
Body Massage Clinic, Waikiki
*Stress busters*

Therapies here include acupressure
sports massage, gentle stretch
manipulation to correct alignment
and *kogao*, a Japanese face massage
that relieves tension and improves
circulation. It's claimed a session
here can sort out stiff backs, sluggish
digestion and stressed minds.
*2155 Kalakaua Avenue*
*+1 808 926 0233*
*bodywaikiki.com*

**⑤**
Spa Halekulani, Waikiki
*Healing hands*

Gray's Beach, in front of the
Halekulani, was once famed
for its therapeutic waters. Today
the healing takes the form of
pampering and is to be found
indoors at the hotel's popular
spa, which offers an array of
traditional treatments.
*2199 Kalia Road*
*+1 808 931 5322*
*halekulani.com*

*Another chorus of
'When I'm Cleaning
Windows' anyone?*

O'ahu has two mountain ranges: Waianae to the west and Ko'olau to the east. These towering behemoths are extinct shield volcanoes that broke through the ocean a few million years ago and built themselves to dramatic heights before becoming dormant giants softened by erosion.

On every hike in these ranges you'll come across something unexpected: ripe *liliko'i* (passionfruit); a boar rustling through grass; a patch of palm trees; a sudden view of the other side of the island; concrete Second World War-era bunkers nestled in the mountainside; or a series of stunning waterfalls.

On O'ahu, hikes depart from surprisingly urban areas and treat trekkers to diverse views. They can take anything from an hour to 12 hours and range from merely strenuous walks to scrambles up steep rock faces. Regardless, it's good to be prepared: wear adequate shoes, bring water, apply sunscreen and insect repellent and pack a few snacks. You should always take your litter home.

Check the weather conditions beforehand: if it has rained recently or wet weather is forecast, expect mud. If you want something reliably steady underfoot, try hikes such as the steep stair climb of Koko Head Crater or Makapu'u Lighthouse Trail, a paved hike that leads to old military bunkers and a view of the lighthouse. They will be drier but busier.

**①**
Kuli'ou'ou Valley Trail
*Steady as she goes*

DISTANCE: 2km round trip
DIFFICULTY: Easy

This trail follows Kuli'ou'ou Stream into Kuli'ou'ou Valley along a path that gradually gives way to uneven terrain. Expect to find small waterfalls that end in pretty pools.

The trailhead is located at the back of Hawaii Kai next to a big Board of Water Supply sign. The entrance is marked by a mailbox. Follow this path for about 300 metres until you come to a sign that points you in two directions: to the right is Kuli'ou'ou Ridge Trail and straight ahead is Kuli'ou'ou Valley Trail. Go straight.

The path continues for just under a kilometre before it ends in an unconquerable tangle of fallen trees. Return the way you came. If required you can cool weary feet in the water along the way but make sure you don't have open wounds: hikers have contracted leptospirosis from streams in Hawaii.

For more of a challenge take the Kuli'ou'ou Ridge Trail. Follow switchbacks to a ridgeline path and finally to stairs that lead to a view of O'ahu. Note that at 8km this is a wholly different prospect to its easy-going neighbour.

**②**
Wa'ahila Ridge Trail
*Ups and downs*

DISTANCE: 4.5km round trip
DIFFICULTY: Moderate

This hike starts at Wa'ahila Ridge State Recreation Area at the top of St Louis Heights, providing the perfect excuse to begin with a picnic amid the park's ironwood pines. But don't overdo it: depending on the season, the trail's strawberry guava trees may be fruiting, making for tasty treats along the way. This hike follows the ridge up and down between Manoa and Palolo valleys and stops at the Kolowalu-Wa'ahila trails junction at the sign that reads "End of Maintained Trail".

By following the signs, hikers can continue further, either down the Kolowalu Trail, which heads into Manoa Valley, or along the Upper Wa'ahila Ridge trail to Mount Olympus, which offers spectacular views. The latter is a hike of about 9km and leads into a protected area where it gets much more difficult and requires ropes.

Forest fruits
——
Keep your
eyes peeled
for wild
guava

(3)
Ka'au Crater Hike
*Deep impact*

DISTANCE: 8km round trip
DIFFICULTY: **Hard**

Unlike the previous two hikes, this
one isn't maintained by the state
and so its entrance is less clear and
its upkeep more irregular. Scratchy
native Hawaiian uluhe ferns grow
along the descent path, making
trousers a sensible choice of attire.
This roughly five-hour journey
takes hikers through tropical forest,
past three waterfalls and along a
ridgeline, leading to views into the
hidden crater and all the way to
Mokoli'i Island.

Its trailhead is found at the
back of Palolo Valley behind a
set of mailboxes at the very end of
Waiomao Road. The hike, marked
by coloured ribbons, entails a walk
along a stream to the first waterfall.
Pause before following the trail
around this and a second waterfall.
Then head up the rocks alongside
a third. The terrain opens up and
the steep ridgeline to the top of the
crater appears. At its peak is the
marshy plain of the crater interior,
source of the three waterfalls you
passed on the way.

Your return leg can be either
back the way you came or along
an alternative path at the top of the
crater, which is less treacherous
but more sloped. It spits hikers out
near the trail's start, muddy, dazed
and satisfied.

READ: *The Hikers Guide to O'ahu*
by Stuart M Ball is a classic
resource that outlines 52 hikes
on the island.

**Trails and
tribulations**
——
The State of Hawaii's Trail and
Access programme, Na Ala
Hele, was set up in 1988 to
protect right of entry to hikes
and historic trails in danger
of disappearing. Head to the
website for details of 43 trails.
*hawaiitrails.ehawaii.gov*

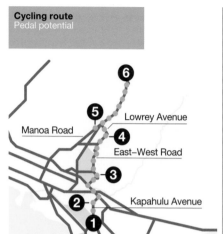

## Cycling route
Pedal potential

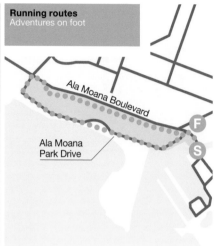

## Running routes
Adventures on foot

Lowrey Avenue

Manoa Road

East–West Road

Kapahulu Avenue

Ala Moana Boulevard

Ala Moana
Park Drive

**1**
Manoa Valley
*Inclined to climb*

STARTING POINT: Ebikes, 3318 Campbell Avenue
DISTANCE: 9.3km

This ride leads to the Lyon Arboretum through the scenic Manoa Valley. Rent an electric bicycle from **1** *Ebikes* and head north to Kapahulu Avenue. After a few minutes you'll reach **2** *Leonard's Bakery*: stop in for *malasadas*: irresistible puffs of deep-fried dough. Continue north and pass under the H1 highway, veering left onto Waialae Avenue. At Kalele Road turn right and cut through the **3** *University of Hawaii at Manoa* campus.

At the Les Murakami Baseball Stadium, take the right fork onto Kalei Road. Follow it round until you reach Dole Street. Turn left and take a right on East–West Road past three buildings by architect IM Pei: Hale Manoa dormitory, Jefferson Hall and Kennedy Theatre (*see page 101*). Continue along East–West Road. Turn left on Pamoa Road and continue until Kolowalu Street. Take a left and then turn right onto East Manoa Road to grab a bite at **4** *Morning Glass Coffee + Café*. Continue along East Manoa and at Lowrey Avenue turn left. Go left at Manoa Road, stopping at **5** *Manoa Heritage Center*, a tudor-style home with native Hawaiian garden (book the $7 tour in advance). Double back on Manoa Road (north), going uphill through the neighbourhoods of Manoa Valley, past the entry point for the Manoa Falls Trail. Park and take the short hike to the falls (1.2km) or keep going until you reach your destination, **6** *Lyon Arboretum*.

**1**
Ala Moana Beach Park
*Beside the seaside*

DISTANCE: 3.5km
GRADIENT: Flat
DIFFICULTY: Easy
HIGHLIGHT: Running along the picturesque shoreline
BEST TIME: Just before sunset

The starting point of this route is easy to reach from hotels in the Waikiki area and takes you around the 30-hectare Ala Moana Beach Park (*ala moana* means "path to the sea"). Start on Ala Moana Boulevard at the bridge spanning the Ala Wai Canal and turn left onto Ala Moana Park Drive. The footpath starts on the left before the road junction and leads past the Waikiki Yacht Club towards Aina Moana, an artificial peninsula made from landfill that's also known as Magic Island.

Continue on the footpath – you will see banyan and monkeypod trees, picnickers and people meditating – along Ala Moana Beach, which has a wading area for children and deepens into a popular swimming area. Until 1934 this was a wetland area of bulrushes and palms once used as a city rubbish dump.

Beyond the Ala Moana Tennis Courts the footpath runs parallel to Ala Moana Park Drive, curving to the right. After passing a pond on your right, take the footpath curving to the right sending you back in the direction you came from, along Ala Moana Boulevard (you will come to a path that's away from the street) until you're back where you started.

---

: **Where to hire a bicycle**
: ———
:
: Besides Ebikes (*ebikeshawaii.com*) we recommend
: Pedal Bike Tours (*pedalbiketours.com*) and The
: Bike Shop Hawaii (*bikeshophawaii.com*).

---

: **Where to buy**
: ———
:
: Our top spots for running gear: The Running Room
: on Kapahulu Avenue (*hawaiirunningroom.com*) and
: Runners Route, in Ala Moana (*run808.com*).

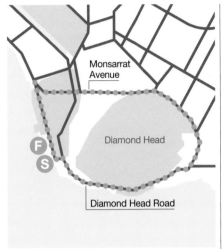

Monsarrat
Avenue

Diamond Head

Diamond Head Road

Ala Wai
Promenade

Date
Street

Ala Wai Boulevard

Waikiki Bay

**2**

Diamond Head
*Coasting up and down*

DISTANCE: 6km
GRADIENT: Long incline, decline
DIFFICULTY: Medium
HIGHLIGHT: Ocean views
BEST TIME: Early mornings

This loop, with its challenging uphill stretch and scenic views over Diamond Head Beach Park, is a favourite with Honolulu's runners. Queen Kapi'olani Regional Park has street parking and is a good place to start your run.

As you head southeast along Diamond Head Road you will pass walled homes clinging to the shore and two small beach parks. From here the road will begin to get steeper. Just beyond a small lighthouse and lookout point, usually easy to spot by the many parked cars, you'll find a stone memorial to pioneering pilot Amelia Earhart, who completed a 3,870km solo flight from Honolulu to Oakland, California, in 1935.

From the right-hand side of the road there is a view of the ocean and you'll likely spot surfers far below riding the diagonal breakers. At Fort Ruger Park, a triangle of greenery marking the site of Honolulu's old artillery defences, veer left and follow Diamond Head Road to the far side of the volcano.

The ascent ends after you pass Kapi'olani Community College, which on Saturdays is thronged with shoppers heading to the KCC Farmers' Market (*see page 38*) held on the site. After this point the road's name changes to Monsarrat Avenue and it begins a long descent through a neighbourhood of homes and shops to the northwest edge of Queen Kapi'olani Regional Park. Turn left on Kalakaua Avenue to complete the loop.

The city's long-distance enthusiasts will usually set off along Diamond Head Road again for at least one more circuit.

**3**

Ala Wai Canal
*Going all the waterway*

DISTANCE: 7km
GRADIENT: Flat
DIFFICULTY: Easy
HIGHLIGHT: Birdlife and boathouses
BEST TIME: Early in the day

This circular route traces the Ala Wai Canal to the Ala Wai Golf Course, following the 2.4km-long tropical estuary, built in the late 1920s, that also doubles as a drainage channel for Honolulu.

Start your run at the steps that lead from Ala Moana Boulevard to the banyan tree-lined Ala Wai Promenade that runs alongside the canal. Early in the morning you'll be accompanied by birdsong and may be joined briefly by canoeists paddling their way along the canal. Cross over the canal on Kalakaua Avenue and continue along the promenade on the other side to McCully Street. Take the footpath at the far end of the car park to continue along the canal.

As you follow the waterway you'll go through Ala Wai Community Park. Next up is the Waikiki Surf Club building, home to Honolulu's members-only organisation of surfers and surfing-canoe racers, founded in 1948. You'll then pass two schools, Ala Wai Elementary with its vast sports field and 'Iolani School with its running track. The footpath then turns into 'Iolani School Driveway.

Continue on until you reach Date Street, then turn right and follow the pavement that runs along the fence bordering the Ala Wai Golf Course. Take a right on Kapahulu Avenue and then turn right again on Ala Wai Boulevard. This final stretch is parallel to the Ala Wai Canal and offers a steady waterside run that will take you all the way back to the starting point.

NEIGHBOURHOOD 01

# Manoa Valley
*Campus art and architecture*

## Walks
— Find your own Honolulu

Don't be put off by the modern dictum that Honolulu was built for the car. Of course, four wheels will help you traverse O'ahu's urban and natural landscapes but it's by foot that many of the secret corners of this bustling Pacific city unfurl. Be it taking in one of the US's oldest Chinatown districts, the architecture of Downtown or the sleepy pockets of Manoa and Kaimuki, the following walks will help you discover Hawaii's capital.

The Manoa Valley stretches from Manoa Falls all the way down to bustling King Street (*Manoa* means "vast" or "deep" in Hawaiian). The fertile valley receives rain almost every day so it was the natural choice for the first sugarcane and coffee plantations in Hawaii. Today the area is home to a slew of cultural institutions and significant Hawaiian architecture that makes it worth taking the short trip from the centre of Honolulu.

This is a neighbourhood of affluent residences – the average cost of a house is more than $1m – and it's also home to the sprawling campus of the University of Hawaii. The student population of about 19,000 is notable for its diversity, with more than half of those enrolled here of Asian or Pacific Islander ancestry. But Manoa is far from a rowdy college town: it's a tranquil, even sleepy place, because most of the undergraduates live – and find their fun – elsewhere.

The campus is well worth a visit because it offers the chance to explore some of Hawaii's finest examples of 20th-century architecture set within a lush natural setting, including buildings by luminaries such as IM Pei and Vladimir Ossipoff. This is a walk for art lovers and those looking to dip into the lesser-known cultural aspects of Honolulu – not to mention the lure of some of the city's most peaceful spots for quiet contemplation.

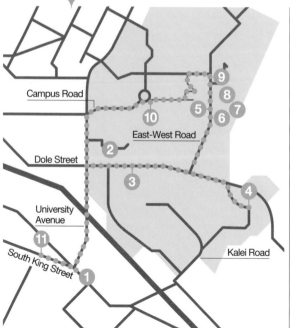

Nature by design
*Manoa Valley walk*

Begin the walk with a flick through the new and used vinyl at ❶ *Hungry Ear Records*, a shop famed for its excellent selection of homegrown vinyl (*see page 52*). Then walk to the intersection of University Avenue, turn right and walk up to the campus.

When you reach the lawned area, look to your right and you'll see the striking ❷ *Bachman Hall*. It was built by Vladimir Ossipoff (*see page 96*) in 1949. On the first floor is

### Getting there
—
Take the CityExpress! bus route A towards UH Manoa from Kapiolani Boulevard just north of Waikiki. To cut out the earlier part of the walk and go straight to the university campus, take bus number 13 from Waikiki to the edge of the campus on Dole Street.

**Address book**

**01** Hungry Ear Records
2615 South King Street
+1 808 262 2175
*hungryear.com*

**02** Bachman Hall
2444 Dole Street
+1 808 956 8111
*manoa.hawaii.edu*

**03** John Young Museum
of Art
2500 Dole Street
+1 808 956 7198
*hawaii.edu/johnyoung-museum*

**04** Kamakakuokalani Center
for Hawaiian Studies
2645 Dole Street
+1 808 956 0555
*manoa.hawaii.edu/hshk*

**05** Kennedy Theatre
1770 East-West Road
+1 808 956 7655
*manoa.hawaii.edu/liveonstage*

**06** Jefferson Hall
Conference Center
1777 East-West Road
+1 808 944 7159
*eastwestcenter.org*

**07** Japanese Garden
1777 East-West Road

**08** Thai Pavilion
1811 East-West Road

**09** Center for Korean Studies
1881 East-West Road
+1 808 956 7041
*hawaii.edu/korea*

**10** The Art Gallery
2535 McCarthy Mall
+1 808 956 6888
*hawaii.edu/art*

**11** Café Maharani
2509 South King Street
+1 808 951 7447
*cafemaharanihawaii.com*

the grand fresco by the French-American painter Jean Charlot, "Relation of Man and Nature in Old Hawaii". Charlot became a professor at the university's school of art following the commission.

Exit onto Dole Street and turn left. You'll soon see the ③ *John Young Museum of Art*. It's the oldest wooden structure on campus and has a fine collection of ceramic, wood and bronze decorative art from the Pacific and Asia.

Keep walking along Dole Street until you get to the Manoa Stream Bridge. On the other side you'll see the pyramid-shaped roof of the ④ *Kamakakuokalani Center for Hawaiian Studies*, recognised as one of the most successful modern interpretations of traditional Hawaiian architecture. Follow the steps down to the Kanewai loʻi waterways, a marvel of engineering and a popular community garden.

Walk back the way you came until you reach East-West Road and turn right. Continue until you reach two imposing concrete buildings on either side of the street: the ⑤ *Kennedy Theatre* and ⑥ *Jefferson Hall Conference Center*. Both were designed by IM Pei and completed in 1963.

Behind the conference centre is a ⑦ *Japanese Garden* by landscape architect Kenzo Ogata. Its three-tiered stream is intended to represent life, which, according to Japanese tradition, begins in turmoil, calms down in adulthood and slows to a serene pace in later life. The Jakuan tea ceremony house is also here.

As you walk back to East-West Road look for the golden ⑧ *Thai Pavilion*, a traditional *sala* dedicated to the East-West Center in 1967 by the king and queen of Thailand and one of just four in existence outside the country. The hardwood structure was built in Thailand and assembled here by Hawaiian artisans.

Continue along East-West Road until you reach the ⑨ *Center for Korean Studies*. The design was inspired by the throne hall at Seoul's Kyongbok Palace and built by South Korean craftsmen in 1979.

Turn left on Maile Way and turn left again at the library. When you hit the park (McCarthy Mall), turn right. After a short walk you will see the ⑩ *The Art Gallery* on your left. Students at the university explore contemporary media – such as sound and digital technologies – alongside traditional visual arts, so the exhibitions are always diverse.

Head along Campus Road back towards University Avenue and turn left. Continue for about 10 minutes to finish your walk at ⑪ *Café Maharani*: this low-key restaurant serves some of the best Indian food in Honolulu.

NEIGHBOURHOOD 02
# Downtown
## *Birthplace of the city*

This is the place to start for anyone interested in getting to grips with Honolulu's architecture and history. It was, after all, the beginning of modern-day Honolulu. Shortly after King Kamehameha I conquered the islands he moved his royal court to the area now called Downtown. When the missionaries arrived in 1820 – an event that set into motion the overthrow of the monarchy and Hawaii's annexation by the US – it was here they built Kawaiaha'o Church using blocks of coral hewn by hand.

The following century brought new methods of construction (and thankfully greater protection for O'ahu's reefs) and a more varied style of architecture, from the copper-roofed stucco of the 1920s to the concrete brutalism of the 1960s. There isn't a lot of contemporary architecture here; Honolulu doesn't have glitzy new museums designed by big-name architects and the current building boom is centred on neighbourhoods such as Kaka'ako and Waikiki.

However, the disparate styles scattered around Downtown represent the story of post-contact Hawaii. From the missionary houses built in 1821 to the 1996 Kohn Pedersen Fox-designed First Hawaiian Center, a journey through this area is also a trip through the historical eras that have shaped the islands. You won't be strolling any beaches or hiking a mountain on this walk but it is nonetheless distinctly Hawaiian.

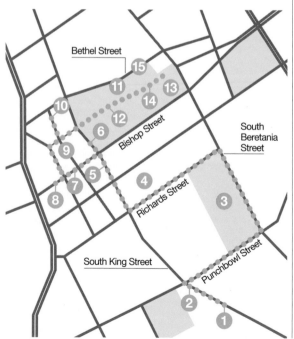

Concrete and coral
*Downtown walk*

Start at the ❶ *Hawaiian mission houses* on South King Street, which were built by Massachusetts missionaries. The oldest house was wood-framed and more relevant to New England winters than Hawaii's climate. Subsequent builds were better suited to the environment and used native materials, including coral. A few metres on at the junction of Punchbowl Street is ❷ *Kawaiaha'o Church*, also built with coral and

completed by missionaries in 1842. Known as the Westminster Abbey of the Pacific, the church still holds weekly services.

From Kawaiaha'o head *mauka* (toward the mountains) on Punchbowl Street and take a left to ❸ *Hawaii State Capitol*, a building designed by John Carl Warnecke and Associates and Belt, Lemmon and Lo, completed in 1969. After the Capitol building, take the first left onto Richards Street to reach Julia Morgan's ❹ *YWCA Building*, built in 1927. If you're hungry, grab lunch at Café Julia, which is named after the architect.

Turn right onto South King Street, where on the junction of Bishop Street you'll see Hawaii's tallest building, ❺ *First Hawaiian Center*, featuring an art gallery programmed by the Honolulu Museum of Art. Across Bishop Street is the equally magnetic ❻ *Financial Plaza of the Pacific*, a collection of brutalist buildings designed in 1968 by Victor Gruen, Lawrence Halprin and Wou and Partners. At the corner of Bishop Street and Merchant Street is the

detailed four-storey **7** *Alexander & Baldwin Building*, created in 1929 by Charles William Dickey and Hart Wood, two of Hawaii's best-known architects. The building is closed to the public but you can see the murals along the Bishop Street portico.

Similarly intricate detailing is at the **8** *Dillingham Transportation Building* down the street (don't miss the frescoed friezes). Follow Queen Street to Fort Street Mall, where the C Brewer Building is a work of Spanish revival architecture by New York architect Hardie Phillip, whose credits also include the Honolulu Museum of Art.

Continue up the mall to Merchant Street. To your right is the **9** *Stangenwald Building*, Hawaii's first commercial high-rise, designed by Dickey in 1901. If you need a pick-me-up, Brue Bar is on the first floor. In the opposite direction is 46 Merchant Street, now **10** *Kumu Kahua Theatre* but known in 1870 as the King Kamehameha V Post Office, the first building in Hawaii to use precast concrete blocks.

Follow Fort Street Mall northeast. Pass South Hotel Street,

and you'll find two weird and wonderful architectural entries: the textural concrete panels and coffin-shaped windows of the **11** *Pantheon Building* (to your left) and the eclectic appearance of the **12** *McCorriston Building* (to your right), built in 1914. Equally delightful is Dickey's Fire Department Central Station from 1934, with its geometric detailing, on nearby South Beretania Street.

Continue further up Fort Street Mall to **13** *Cathedral Basilica of Our Lady of Peace*, the oldest cathedral in continuous use in the US. It was completed in 1843 but unlike their Protestant contemporaries the Catholics covered the church's coral blocks with beige stucco to resemble European cathedrals.

For a slice of Honolulu's 20th-century architecture, drop in to the supposedly haunted **14** *Blaisdell Hotel*, which long ago took its last guests but still thrums with activity as home to artsy small businesses such as Le Crêpe Café. Round off your walk with a well-earned beer at **15** *Proof Public House*, a relaxed pub tucked away down a side road.

### Getting there

To make the trip from Waikiki take buses 2, 4, 13, 19, 20, 42 or the E Express to reach Downtown. If you're driving to the first location there is metered parking along Kawaiaha'o and South streets and a pay car park located at the corner of South and Queen streets.

## Address book

**01 Hawaiian mission houses**
553 South King Street
+1 808 447 3910
*missionhouses.org*

**02 Kawaiaha'o Church**
957 Punchbowl Street
+1 808 469 3000
*kawaiahao.org*

**03 Hawaii State Capitol**
415 South Beretania Street
+1 808 586 0221
*governor.hawaii.gov*

**04 YWCA Building**
1040 Richards Street
+1 808 538 7061
*ywcaoahu.org*

**05 First Hawaiian Center**
999 Bishop Street
+1 808 532 8701
*honolulumuseum.org*

**06 Financial Plaza of the Pacific**
130 Merchant Street

**07 Alexander & Baldwin Building**
822 Bishop Street
+1 808 525 6611
*alexanderbaldwin.com*

**08 Dillingham Transportation Building**
735 Bishop Street

**09 Stangenwald Building**
119 Merchant Street

**10 Kumu Kahua Theatre**
46 Merchant Street
+1 808 536 4441
*kumukahua.org*

**11 Pantheon Building**
1102-1122 Fort Street Mall

**12 McCorriston Building**
1107 Fort Street Mall

**13 Cathedral Basilica of Our Lady of Peace**
1184 Bishop Street
+1 808 536 7036
*cathedralofourladyof peace.com*

**14 Blaisdell Hotel**
1152 Fort Street Mall

**15 Proof Public House**
1154 Fort Street Mall
+1 808 537 3080
*proofpublichouse.com*

NEIGHBOURHOOD 03
# Kaimuki
*Laidback suburbia*

A couple of kilometres inland from Waikiki, Kaimuki is a mellow residential neighbourhood with a burgeoning food scene and a charm rooted in its plantation-style homes. Its name is usually translated from Hawaiian as "ti-root oven"; some say that this is due to a legend that Hawaii's mythical sprites, the *menehune*, favoured the site as a place to cook. One of Honolulu's earliest subdivisions, Kaimuki's rich and diverse history includes a time when ostriches kept by King Kalakaua's court physician roamed on its slopes.

Until the 1960s the district was the nearest thing Honolulu had to a main hub, with electric trolleys that stopped at Koko Head Avenue bringing military personnel and islanders to its shops. But when O'ahu's first freeway, Interstate H1, was completed it bypassed the neighbourhood and the area hasn't changed much since. Bygone landmarks abound, such as the Queens Theater, opened in 1936 and closed in 1987, whose still-standing sign is a distinguishing feature of Waialae Avenue.

We suggest a stroll along the quiet residential streets towards Diamond Head, taking in the plantation-style houses with Asian flair sitting alongside newer two-storey homes. Along Waialae, old businesses mingle with new and there's a thriving food scene, making it a perfect spot to round off your trek.

Coffee and culture
*Kaimuki walk*

Begin with a fresh cup of coffee at **1** *The Curb*: it's a no-frills café wedged between a 7-Eleven and a pho restaurant but it has the best coffee in town. Exit onto Waialae Avenue and turn left. Take the second right onto 12th Avenue and **2** *Koko Head Café* will be on your left, a bustling brunch spot run by chef Lee Anne Wong. The cornflake French toast should help you stay the course.

On the other side of the car park is **3** *Crack Seed Store,* where owner Kon Ping Young has peddled a popular Hawaiian-Chinese snack called Crack Seed – "The old-school kind, not the stuff you get at Long's"– since 1979. Ask him to scoop you a spoonful of *li hing mui* (salty dried plum) seed while you peruse jars of mango seed and cuttlefish.

Take Koko Head Avenue on the right towards Diamond Head until you reach a white Spanish Mission-style building. This is **4** *Kaimuki Fire Station*, built in 1924 and designed by architect GR Miller; it is still in use and rumoured to host a ghost. Continue left on Pahoa Avenue and take the first right on Ocean View Drive. Following this will get you to the entrance of Pu'u O Kaimuki, a mini park with a view of the ocean, Koko Head Crater, Diamond Head Crater and downtown Honolulu. Descend the opposite side of the hill and walk along Pahoa Avenue and take a right onto 10th Avenue. By staying in the residential area you'll get a good feel for its signature plantation-style homes and pass ginger plants

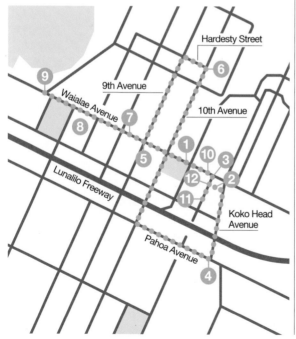

and banana, avocado, mango and fragrant plumeria trees.

For lunch and a cool treat in the middle of the day there are two great independent options of very different persuasions near 10th Avenue. If you are hankering for organic vegetables, try ⑤ *Leahi Health* on Waialae Avenue. Get the rainbow taco – a naan with bright 'slaw, goji berries and almonds – and a Poi Boy smoothie made with pounded taro. For something a little meatier head back onto 10th Avenue to ⑥ *Your Kitchen*, a plate-lunch spot where you can enjoy braised pork belly and panko-crusted egg or sample the shave ice and vanilla ice cream.

Back on Waialae Avenue, ⑦ *The Public Pet* is a boutique for furry friends offering aloha-print kerchiefs and raw-food dog treats, as well as finds ranging from cat nip and organic pet shampoos to ceramics. Continue further along the street to ⑧ *St Patrick Church*. The looming white Romanesque structure, built in 1929, was designed by architect RA Fishbourne and finished with two bells imported from Brussels.

A few blocks further is ⑨ *Honolulu Aiki Dojo*. It was the first built outside Japan for aikido and comes to life in the morning and evening for classes (it's shut between 10.00 and 17.30 most days). Visitors are welcome to watch but remove your shoes and don't take photos.

For a browse through vintage Hawaiiana, head back the way you came on Waialae to ⑩ *Surf'n'Hula*, owned by collector and Kaimuki native Kenneth Furukawa. The shop is crammed with surf trophies and souvenir tikis as well as vintage aloha shirts that are, naturally, its best sellers.

Dinner is at ⑪ *12th Avenue Grill*, offering Hawaiian-infused new-American cuisine. Sip a cocktail at the bar or grab a table and order duck over pink-peppercorn tagliatelle tangled with *kabocha*, tomatoes and a lemon-ricotta sauce.

End the day at ⑫ *Via Gelato* along with what seems like most of Kaimuki's population. If an evening on the town beckons, perk up with owner Melissa Bow's affogato: a shot of perfectly brewed espresso poured over two scoops of your choice.

### Getting there

Take eastbound bus 9 from Ala Moana Center or eastbound bus 1 from King Street to Waialae Avenue and Koko Head Avenue. There's metered street parking or two paid car parks on 12th Avenue. Free parking on streets off Waialae is available but limited.

## Address book

**01** The Curb
3538 Waialae Avenue
+1 808 315 1912
*thecurbco.com*

**02** Koko Head Café
1145C 12th Avenue
+1 808 732 8920
*kokoheadcafe.com*

**03** Crack Seed Store
1156 Koko Head Avenue
+1 808 737 1022

**04** Kaimuki Fire Station
971 Koko Head Avenue
+1 808 523 4669

**05** Leahi Health
3441 Waialae Avenue
+1 808 388 4181
*leahihealth.com*

**06** Your Kitchen
1423 10th Avenue
+1 808 203 7685

**07** The Public Pet
3422 Waialae Avenue
*thepublicpet.com*

**08** St Patrick Church
1124 7th Avenue
+1 808 732 5565

**09** Honolulu Aiki Dojo
3224 Waialae Avenue
+1 808 737 7133

**10** Surf'n'Hula
3588 Waialae Avenue
*surfnhula.com*

**11** 12th Avenue Grill
1120 12th Avenue
+1 808 732 9469
*12thavegrill.com*

**12** Via Gelato
1142 12th Avenue
+1 808 832 2800
*viagelatohawaii.com*

NEIGHBOURHOOD 04
# Chinatown
*Cultural rebirth*

On a map, Chinatown barely registers in its spot just a few blocks across from Honolulu Harbor. But the neighbourhood is one of the city's most walkable and increasingly popular, packing an outsized cultural punch. Though much original character was lost in the fire of 1900, its narrow streets are still a feast for the senses, especially at midday when the area from Ala Moana Boulevard to North Beretania Street becomes one big market.

Unlike its counterparts on the US mainland, Honolulu's Chinatown has always been multi-ethnic. From the 1830s it was a hub for Chinese immigrants but also Vietnamese, Japanese, South Koreans, Filipinos and others who arrived to work on O'ahu's plantations and railroads. Today you can find Cantonese dim sum, Vietnamese pho, Moroccan tagine, Laotian fried chicken and Ethiopian *shiro*, all within minutes of one another.

Chinatown always catered to folks fresh off the boat and, with the influx of sailors, by the Second World War the area had become the red-light district. Today the bars, brothels and tattoo parlours have given way to a food-and-fashion renaissance typified by refined ventures such as modern-Vietnamese restaurant The Pig & the Lady, tiki-wear specialist Roberta Oaks and bean-to-bar confectioner Madre Chocolate. We explore the oft-overlooked gems and the traditional culture on which the area was built.

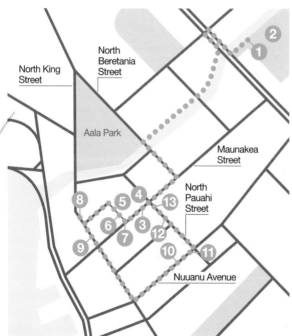

North King Street

North Beretania Street

Aala Park

Maunakea Street

North Pauahi Street

Nuuanu Avenue

Food and history
*Chinatown walk*

Begin your walk at the ornate Buddhist ❶ *Kuan Yin Temple*, devoted to the female *bodhisattva* of mercy. Worshippers regularly light incense or leave fresh flowers and fruit as offerings at the foot of the golden statue. The serenity and evocative aromas will ensure a peaceful start to the day. Directly behind the temple is ❷ *Foster Botanical Garden*, where you can visit the Bodhi tree said to be descended from the offspring of the sacred fig tree under which Buddha attained enlightenment.

From the garden, head northwest and cross North Vineyard Boulevard at Aala Street, then do a slight U-turn and take a right onto the river path *makai* (toward the ocean) into the heart of Chinatown. Cross over the river onto North Beretania Street and continue until you turn right onto Maunakea Street. Where it meets North Pauahi Street on the corner you'll find intricate but inexpensive fresh-flower lei at ❸ *MP Lei Shop*.

Across the street, Maunakea Marketplace is home to mostly imported kitsch but there are two worthwhile stop-offs. ❹ *Mickey Café* is one of the few places on the island that offers *gai daan jai* (egg puffs): a delicious, waffle-like snack covered in pancake batter. On the market's second floor you can get a sense of the community's O'ahu story at the ❺ *Hawaiian Chinese Multicultural Museum and Archives*.

There are two more places rich in history at the corner of Maunakea and North Hotel streets. The ❻ *Wo Fat Building*

## Getting there

Take buses 12, 20 or 42 and get off at the intersection at North Beretania and Smith streets. From there walk along Maunakea Street to North Vineyard Boulevard. If you're driving, there's free parking at Foster Botanical Garden or plenty of paid car parks in Chinatown itself.

was home to Wo Fat, Honolulu's oldest restaurant (although it's now closed) and a spot cheekily referenced by *Hawaii Five-O*'s scriptwriters (the cop show's arch villain was named after it). Across the street is **7** *Chinatown Police Station* where Chang Apana, the real-life inspiration for fictional 1920s detective Charlie Chan, once did his sleuthing.

Head northwest on North Hotel Street and then left along Kekaulike Street, lined with dragon-fruit and prawn sellers. Take a right onto North King Street to visit **8** *Yat Tung Chow Noodle Factory* for fresh noodles and wonton wrappers. Across the street at O'ahu Market, established in 1904, pigs' heads peer from coolers and ducks hang on hooks; fresh fish is popular but you can buy almost any animal part here. For even odder bites head south on North King Street to **9** *Fook Sau Tong* where Dr Suen Hang Yee sells mountain roaches and sea dragons, which are made into soup or tea.

Continue south past The Pig & the Lady (*see page 32*) until

you reach Nuuanu Avenue. Stop for a chat with the agents at **10** *World Wide Travel Service*, an old-fashioned travel agency. They can give you a crash course in Hawaiian history. At **11** *Art Treasures Gallery* owner Fong Chan is a font of knowledge on antiquities, from lime pots in Vietnamese culture to the history of Chinese inkstones.

Turn left on North Pauahi Street. Make a pit-stop at **12** *Char Hung Sut*, run by third-generation Chinese-Hawaiians Bruce and Barry Mao. Here you'll find Chinatown's best *manapua* (char siu pork-filled baos), the perfect bite to set you up for a visit to **13** *Wing Shave Ice & Ice Cream* which, despite sharing an address with MP Lei Shop, has its entrance on North Pauahi Street. Try a scoop of *kurosawa* ice cream (vanilla, matcha and strawberry) or *li hing miu* (salty dried plum) and mango. Owner Miller Wing Royer grew up around here and is just one of a new wave of restaurateurs ensuring this old neighbourhood continues its cultural rise.

## Address book

**01** Kuan Yin Temple
170 North Vineyard Boulevard

**02** Foster Botanical Garden
180 North Vineyard Boulevard
+1 808 522 7060

**03** MP Lei Shop
1145 Maunakea Street
+1 808 531 3206

**04** Mickey Café
1120 Maunakea Street
+1 808 462 8626
*mickeycafe.com*

**05** Hawaiian Chinese Multicultural Museum and Archives
1120 Maunakea Street
+1 808 285 8316

**06** Wo Fat Building
103 North Hotel Street

**07** Chinatown Police Station
79 North Hotel Street

**08** Yat Tung Chow Noodle Factory
150 North King Street
+1 808 531 7982

**09** Fook Sau Tong
112 North King Street
+1 808 531 6680

**10** World Wide Travel Service
1120 Nuuanu Avenue
+1 808 533 3691

**11** Art Treasures Gallery
1136 Nuuanu Avenue
+1 808 536 7789
*arttreasureshawaii.com*

**12** Char Hung Sut
64 North Pauahi Street
+1 808 538 3335
*charhungsutrestaurant.com*

**13** Wing Shave Ice & Ice Cream
1145 Maunakea Street
+1 808 536 4929

# Beyond the city
—— Day trips

What would a guide to Honolulu be without tips on how to enjoy some of the sites that lie outside the city limits? Exploring small towns, roadside restaurants and uncrowded beaches is part of the attraction of a visit to O'ahu. Here are two destinations where you can enjoy a swim in clear water followed by a tipple, while also picking up a few items for your wardrobe.

01

02

03

DAY TRIP 01
# Kailua
*Beyond the sea*

On the eastern side of O'ahu sits Kailua, a once-sleepy town of 39,000 residents. Today it's a magnet for tourists and Honolulu residents alike thanks to its pristine beaches: Kailua and Kalama. But Kailua is also home to an eclectic band of entrepreneurs who have opened shops, shave-ice stands and cafés and are showing that this town has much more to offer than simply sand and sea.

**1**

Lanikai Brewing Company
*Fruity flavours*

Lanikai Brewing was launched in 2014 through a Kickstarter campaign. Brewmaster Steve Haumschild makes beers with Hawaiian *jabong* (pomelo) fruit, hibiscus flowers and honey, which he supplies to grocery shops, bars and restaurants around O'ahu. Lanikai's tasting room opens on weekends.
*175 Hamakua Drive*
*lanikaibrewing.com*

**2**

Aloha Beach Club
*Hawaiian style*

Kahana Kalama and his co-founder Billy Wickens opened this shop in 2015, selling surfboards, eyewear, hats, Oxford shirts and board shorts from in-house brands Shoots and Aloha Beach Club.
*131 Hekili Street, Suite 108*
*alohabeachclub.com*

Kailua Bay

**8**

Kihapai Street

Uluniu Street

Kailua Beach

**8**

**7**

**4**

**5**

Helkili Street

**6**

**3**

**2**

**1**

Hamakua Drive

01—02 Lanikai Brewing
Company
03 Aloha Beach Club
04—05 The Local Hawaii
06 Oliver

*Cool business*

Shave ice is a typically Hawaiian treat

04  05

06

### Breakfast club
———
Moke's Bread & Breakfast is a family-run institution opened in 1999. A great crowd-pleaser is the fluffy *liliko'i* (passionfruit) pancakes made from a generations-old recipe and covered in a creamy sauce. Open from 06.30 to 14.00.
*mokeskailua.com*

01 — 03    Olive Boutique
04 — 07    ChadLou's
08    Oliver
09 — 10    Kailua Beach Park and
Kalama Beach Park

01

02

03    04

05    06

**3**

The Local Hawaii
*Ice cold*

This popular shave-ice counter
inside Aloha Beach Club offers
17 syrup toppings created
from Hawaiian-grown fruit:
guava, pineapple, lychee, mango,
strawberry and many more. It
also sells a delicious range of
handmade sodas.
*Unit 108, 131 Hekili Street*
*thelocalhawaii.com*

07

08

Kailua and Kalama
—
Rest easy at beaches free from sellers

09

**How to get there**

The 20km trip from Honolulu to Kailua takes 40 minutes by car. Go north on the Pali Highway (Route 61) to Route 72 and exit at Kailua Road. Alternatively, it's a 45-minute bus ride (routes 56, 57 and 57A) from Ala Moana Center.

10

Olive Boutique
*Island fashion*

Kailua native Ali McMahon's chic womenswear shop stocks clothing from brands such as Ella Moss, Boys + Arrows and Splendid.
*43 Kihapai Street*
*+1 808 263 9919*
*iheartolive.com*

Oliver
*Family affair*

Parker Moosman's shop sits just two doors down from his wife Ali McMahon's and specialises in Hawaiian menswear brands such as Salvage Public and Eroix.
*49 Kihapai Street*
*+1 808 261 6587*
*oliverhawaii.com*

ChadLou's
*Coffee and cream*

At Sheila Lou and Matt Rosete's café you can order coffee or one of life's great pleasures: an ice cream sandwich made from cookies and Honolulu-made Dave's Ice Cream.
*45 Kihapai Street*
*+1 808 263 7930*
*chadlous.com*

Aloha Superette
*Ocean colours*

Jennifer Binney started her **Samudra** line of tropics-themed pouches in 2011. Four years later she opened this shop to sell the colourful products.
*438 Uluniu Street*
*+1 808 261 1011*
*alohasuperette.com*

Kailua Beach Park and Kalama Beach Park
*Free and easy*

Thanks to the Honolulu City Council's decision in 2012 to ban most commercial activity, Kailua's tout-free beaches are perfect for walking, running, swimming, surfing and lounging in the sun.

DAY TRIP 02
# North Shore
*Northern soul*

The town of Hale'iwa (population 4,000) lies one hour's drive from Honolulu on O'ahu's North Shore. It was here in Waimea Bay where the first westerners to visit O'ahu island – aboard Captain Cook's ship – made a brief stop to replenish fresh-water supplies. Today the town, the name of which means "house of the frigatebird", is best known for its proximity to Seven-Mile Miracle: a stretch of coastline where winter swells attract top surfers.

**①**

Lanikai Juice
*Juicy fruits*

Pablo Gonzalez opened his first Lanikai Juice shop in 1997 and uses fresh Hawaiian produce (organic, when possible). Stevia and honey are the only sweeteners added to juices, smoothies and açaí and *pitaya* (dragonfruit) bowls.
*66-215 Kamehameha Highway*
*+1 808 637 7774*
*lanikaijuice.com*

**②**

Hawaiian Shochu Company
*Crystal clear*

Ken and Yumiko Hirata produce limited quantities of Namihana *shochu* from sweet potatoes grown in Hawaii at their micro-distillery on the outskirts of Hale'iwa.
*66-542 Hale'iwa Road (entrance on Paalaa Road)*
*+1 808 234 4162*

**③**

No 808
*Informal fashion*

John and Cappy Esguerra's shop stocks casual menswear, womenswear and eyewear. Its brands include John's own Quality Peoples clothing line, Japanese labels Kapital and Engineered Garments, and New York's Saturdays NYC.
*66-165 Kamehameha Highway*
*+1 808 312 1579*
*number808.com*

01

03

02    04

Surf's up
——
Sunset Beach is known for its big winter waves

05

06

08

07

01, 03    Lanikai Juice
02    Welcome to Hale'iwa
04, 05, 08    North Shore beaches
06    Hawaiian Shochu Company
07    No 808
09, 11    Greenroom Hawaii
10    Storto's Sandwich Shoppe

10

09    11

Greenroom Hawaii
*Home decor*

The North Shore outpost for co-
founders Naoki Kamayachi and Jun
Yoshimura sells prints and clothing
including N Mii shorts and Salvage
Public and Banks shirts.
*66-111 Kamehameha Highway*
*+1 808 924 4404*
*greenroomhawaii.com*

Storto's Sandwich Shoppe
*Wake and bake*

Pam and Brian Jett's shop bakes
bread daily for its sandwiches,
which are all named after popular
North Shore surf breaks.
*66-215 Kamehameha Highway*
*+1 808 637 6633*
*stortoshaleiwa.com*

Kono's
*Breakfast bonanza*

Visit for the breakfast bombers –
burritos with potatoes, eggs and
cheese – and sandwiches stuffed
with slow-cooked pork.
*66-250 Kamehameha Highway*
*+1 808 637 9211*
*kaluapork.com*

⑦
Hale'iwa Bowls
*Bowled over*

Açaí bowls, smoothies and other
fruit-focused fare are the draw at
this small roadside takeaway stand.
*66-082 Kamehameha Highway*
*haleiwabowls.com*

⑧
Snow Factory and Il Gelato
*World-class ice cream*

The Snow Factory truck in the car
park at the junction of Paalaa Road
and Kamehameha Highway makes
its "frozen cotton candy" from fruit,
juices and milk. Nearby there's
also Il Gelato, run by Carpigiani
Gelato University graduate Dirk
Koeppenkastrop, captain of the US
team that competed at the World
Gelato Championships.
*66-250 Kamehameha Highway*
*+1 808 637 7100*
*ilgelato-hawaii.com*

⑨
VJ's North Shore Dogs & Burgers
*Meat and greet*

In the car park next to Justin and
Jenny Javier's meat shop, VJ's Butcher
Block, sits their takeaway food shack,
VJ's North Shore Dogs & Burgers,
which serves beef made from grass-
fed cows on Moloka'i Island.
*66-470 Kamehameha Highway*
*+1 808 637 6328*

03

01

04

05

06

02

Jump for joy
—
Leaping from the rocks at Waimea Bay is popular

09

10

 **10**
Beaches
*Wave power*

Even if you don't surf you can watch from the shore at Banzai Pipeline and Sunset Beach (*see page 114*) as the surfers tear through the towering winter swells. In summer Waimea Bay's waves are small, making this a popular swimming and sunbathing spot. Just 3km to the south is Laniakea Beach, a haven for sea turtles.

 **11**
Hale'iwa Farmers' Market
*Farm fresh*

On Thursdays from midday at the Hale'iwa Farmers' Market you'll find owners of nearby farms and others from further afield selling fresh produce. It's a short walk to scenic Waimea Falls, also known as Waihi Falls.
*59-864 Kamehameha Highway*
*+1 808 388 9696*
*farmloversmarkets.com*

### How to get there
—
The 50km drive from Honolulu to Hale'iwa takes one hour. Go west on Interstate H1 and north on Interstate H2. Continue on Wilikina Drive to Route 803 north. Turn right at Kaukonahua Road and take the Kamehameha Highway into town.

07

08

# Resources
— Inside knowledge

By now you will have realised that although Honolulu is blessed with some of the world's most stunning shoreline, there's much more to the city than surf and sand. So far we have told you about the Vladimir Ossipoff-designed landmarks, how to read Hawaiian words and where to find the freshest *poke* or a satisfying mai tai nightcap.

In this section you will read about navigating the city on bus, bike or taxi. We also have suggestions for outdoor and indoor activities, a list of our favourite events and a selection of tunes for the perfect relaxing soundtrack to your trip.

## Transport
### Get around town

01 **Car:** A vehicle is still the best way to get around, despite the jammed streets. You'll find six car-rental companies at Honolulu International Airport and most also have Waikiki outposts.
*hawaii.gov/hnl;*
*hawaiismartcarrentals.com*

02 **Bus:** These distinctive yellow-and-orange vehicles connect the city centre and surrounding suburbs. One-way fares cost $2.50 or you can buy a $35 four-day unlimited pass.
*thebus.org*

03 **Waikiki Trolley:** The hop-on, hop-off service covers five routes that will get you around the retail and historic districts. A one-day pass for one route is $25; to access all routes the cost is $45.
*waikikitrolley.com*

04 **Taxi:** Cabs are easy to flag. Charley's Taxi is a solid option that has been operating a fleet of taxis, vans and limos since 1938. Or book EcoCab's petrol-electric hybrid cars.
*charleystaxi.com;*
*ecocabhawaii.com*

05 **Electric bicycles:** Take in the sights at a slower pace. Ebikes Hawaii rents Haibike and A2B electric bikes and Brompton bikes for $25 to $80 a day.
*ebikeshawaii.com*

06 **Trains:** Honolulu's elevated rail line is behind schedule but when it's completed – slated for 2021 – the $6.5bn project will feature driverless cars and 32km of track from Kapole, in west Oʻahu, to Waikiki.
*honolulutransit.org*

07 **Flights:** It's easy to get to Hawaii's other islands. Island Air has more than 165 weekly flights between Oʻahu, Maui and more, while Mokulele Airlines connects Oʻahu, Maui, Molokaʻi and Hawaii. Hawaiian Airlines flies to six of the main islands, including Kauai.
*islandair.com;*
*mokuleleairlines.com;*
*hawaiianairlines.com*

## Vocabulary
### Local lingo

This list of terms will help you navigate the linguistic landscape.

01 **A hui hou:** until we meet again
02 **Aloha:** hello, love, regards
03 **Bumbai:** eventually, or else
04 **Choke:** a lot of something
05 **Da kine:** a thing, you know, whatchamacallit
06 **Grinds:** food
07 **Hana hou:** do it again!
08 **Mahalo:** thank you
09 **Shoots:** sure, I understand

## Honolulu playlist
### Five top tunes

01 **Andy Cummings, 'Waikiki':** Classic *hapa-haole* (mixed Caucasian-Hawaiian) song written by Honolulu-born Cummings in 1946. An ode to Waikiki and its "magic beside the sea", the song is still widely performed today.

02 **Gabby Pahinui, 'Hiʻilawe':** Folk hero guitarist and singer Gabby "Pops" Pahinui was an important figure in the renaissance of Hawaiian culture in the 1970s. His classic song was first recorded in 1946 and appears on the soundtrack of 2011 film *The Descendants*.

03 **Nohelani Cypriano, 'Lihue':** Honolulu's queen of Hawaiian funk with a whiff of disco.

04 **Israel Kamakawiwoʻole, 'Somewhere Over the Rainbow':** Taken from his 1993 album *Facing Future* – the bestselling Hawaiian album of all time – this reggae-inflected ukulele track made a worldwide star of Iz, the late Kaimuki-raised musician and independence activist.

05 **Mr Carmack, 'Likelike Highway':** Pronounced "lick-eh lick-eh highway", this electronic track by Honolulu-based DJ Aaron Carmack is named after Route 63, which runs through Oʻahu's Koʻolau Range.

## Best events
What to see

## Sunny days
The great outdoors

## Rainy days
Weather-proof activities

**01** Chinese New Year, various venues: The annual celebrations in Chinatown include fireworks, plus the Narcissus Queen Pageant. *January or February*

**02** Pow! Wow! Hawaii, various venues: Hundreds of graffiti artists transform the resurgent Kaka'ako district for this vibrant festival. *February, powwowhawaii.com*

**03** Honolulu Festival, various venues: Large cultural jamboree with street parades and musical performances. *March, honolulufestival.com*

**04** Hawaii Food and Wine Festival, various venues: Two-week epicurean fest co-founded by Hawaiian chefs Roy Yamaguchi and Alan Wong. *Date varies annually, hawaiifoodandwinefestival.com*

**05** Spam Jam, Kalakaua Avenue: A celebration of Hawaii's devotion to the tinned, processed meat. *April, spamjamhawaii.com*

**06** Hawaii International Film Festival, various venues: Hawaii's newest cinematic gems and world cinema. *April, hiff.org*

**07** Bon Dance Season, various venues: A series of traditional Japanese Bon dance events celebrating departed souls. *June to September*

**08** Aloha Festivals, various venues: This cultural affair on O'ahu features multiple events incorporating street parades and concerts. *September, alohafestivals.com*

**09** Vans Triple Crown of Surfing, North Shore: A series of key pro-surf contests held in the winter swells. *November to December, worldsurfleague.com*

**10** Eat the Street, 1011 Ala Moana Boulevard: Quality street food from sellers along the Kewalo Harbor waterfront. *Last Friday of every month, eatthestreethawaii.com*

While a sunny day with tradewinds may blow you in the direction of one of Honolulu's white-sand beaches – and you should follow this impulse – there are other options to consider when the sun is at its zenith. Regardless, apply sunscreen.

**01** Learn to surf, Waikiki: Professional longboard surfer Kelia Moniz and her brothers learned to surf in Waikiki while their parents, legendary big-wave rider Tony Moniz and his wife Tammy, set up Faith Surf School. Today its home base is in front of Outrigger Waikiki Beach Resort. A lesson from the Moniz family's company will get you riding a wave inside iconic breaks such as Queens and Canoes. *faithsurfschool.com*

**02** Koko Crater Botanical Garden, Hawaii Kai: The basin of Koko Crater, a 100,000-year-old volcanic cone, has the ideal hot, arid climate for plants such as the Sonoran palmetto and golden barrel cactus. Grab a map from the entrance (on Kokonani Street), and follow the 3km dirt path that passes a plumeria grove, then goes on through sections dedicated to Africa and Madagascar, Hawaii and the Americas. Picnic tables are available but bring water. *honolulu.gov*

**03** Manoa Heritage Center, Manoa: This historic estate is home to Honolulu's last intact *heiau*, or pre-Christian place of worship. A tour here (Monday to Friday; advanced reservation only) includes the *heiau* as well as gardens featuring indigenous plants and "canoe plants" brought to the islands by Polynesian seafarers. There is also a Tudor-style residence, built in 1911, where Mary Cooke, who founded this non-profit organisation, lives. *manoaheritagecenter.org*

Depending on the season, rain in Hawaii may last a few minutes or several hours. Either way, a foreboding forecast is a good excuse to appreciate the indoor activities Honolulu has to offer.

**01** Doris Duke Theatre, Downtown: Tucked away on the *mauka* (mountain) side of the Honolulu Museum of Art is the Doris Duke Theatre, a 280-seat space where a broad selection of independent, documentary and international films are screened. The theatre's projectionist also works the small concession stand in the lobby and usually introduces the film, providing a background on the director and explaining the significant cultural references. *honolulumuseum.org*

**02** Afternoon tea at Halekulani, Waikiki: There is romance in enjoying a stormy day near the sea. At the Halekulani, rain or shine, afternoon tea is served at The Veranda – a six-table setting with doors open to the ocean breeze – from 15.00 to 17.30. The Classic Afternoon Tea includes a tower of sandwiches and pastries along with a pot of tea, while Champagne Afternoon Tea takes the classic menu and tops it off with champagne and strawberries with cream. *halekulani.com*

**03** Get cooking, various venues: Make your own chocolate bar on Wednesdays and Fridays at Madre Chocolate in Chinatown, which sources cacao beans from Hawaii and overseas. Learn the craft, from fermentation to final product, then create your own with flavours such as Hawaiian sea salt or caramelised ginger. CookSpace in Kaka'ako, meanwhile, offers tastings and classes in hand-cut pasta or sweet-making. *madrechocolate.com; cookspacehawaii.com*

# About Monocle
## — Step inside

In 2007, Monocle was launched as a monthly magazine briefing on global affairs, business, culture, design and much more. We believed there was a globally minded audience of readers who were hungry for opportunities and experiences beyond their national borders.

Today Monocle is a complete media brand with print, audio and online elements – not to mention our expanding network of shops and cafés. Besides our London HQ we have seven international bureaux in New York, Toronto, Istanbul, Singapore, Tokyo, Zürich and Hong Kong. We continue to grow and flourish and at our core is the simple belief that there will always be a place for a print brand that is committed to telling fresh stories and sending photographers on assignments.

**❶**
International bureaux
*Boots on the ground*

We have an HQ in London and call upon firsthand reports from our contributors in more than 35 cities around the world. We also have seven international bureaux. For this travel guide, Asia bureau chief Fiona Wilson, Asia editor at large Kenji Hall and Toronto bureau chief Tomos Lewis donned their aloha shirts and jetted to Honolulu. They also called on the assistance of writers and researchers on the island to ensure we have covered the best retail, food, hospitality and entertainment on offer. The aim is to make you, the reader, feel like a local when you visit.

**❷**
Print
*Committed to the page*

MONOCLE is published 10 times a year. We have stayed loyal to our belief in quality print with two new seasonal publications: THE FORECAST, packed with key insights into the year ahead, and THE ESCAPIST, our summer travel-minded magazine. To sign up visit *monocle.com/subscribe*. Since 2013 we have also been publishing books, like this one, in partnership with Gestalten.

**On air**
—
Our radio studios are on site at Midori House

# Join us

There are lots of ways to be part of the ever-expanding Monocle world whether in print, online, or on your radio. We'd love to have you join the club.

## 01
## Read the magazine

You can buy Monocle magazine at newsstands in more than 60 countries around the world, or get yourself an annual subscription at *monocle.com.*

## 02
## Listen to Monocle 24

You can tune in to Monocle 24 radio live via our free app, at *monocle.com* or on any internet-enabled radio. Or download our shows from iTunes or SoundCloud to keep informed as you travel the globe.

## 03
## Subscribe to the Monocle Minute

Sign up today to the Monocle Minute, our free daily news and views email, at *monocle.com.* Our website is also where you'll find a world of free films, our online shop and updates about everything that we are up to.

**③**
Radio
*Sound approach*

Monocle 24 is our round-the-clock radio station that was launched in 2011. It delivers global news and shows covering foreign affairs, urbanism, business, culture, food and drink, design and print media. When you find yourself in Honolulu you can listen to *The Monocle Daily*, our morning news programme that is the perfect way to start the day in the US; Monocle 24's editors, presenters and guests set the agenda in international news and business. All of our shows are available as podcasts to enjoy on your travels; go to iTunes, SoundCloud or *monocle.com* to build your playlist.

**④**
Online
*Digital delivery*

We also have a dynamic website: *monocle.com.* As well as it being the place to hear Monocle 24, we use the site to present our films, which are beautifully shot and edited by our in-house team and provide a fresh perspective on our stories. Check out the films celebrating the cities that make up our Travel Guide Series before you explore the rest of the site.

**⑤**
Retail and cafés
*Good taste*

Via our shops in Hong Kong, Toronto, New York, Tokyo, London and Singapore we sell products that cater to our readers' tastes and are produced in collaboration with brands we believe in. We also have cafés in Tokyo and London serving coffee and Japanese delicacies among other things – and we are set to expand this arm of our business.

# MONOCLE

Keeping an eye and an ear on the world

**Writers**
Timothy A Schuler
Laura Blears
Martha Cheng
Kenji Hall
Stephanie Han
Anna Harmon
Dale Hope
Jerry Hopkins
Pegge Hopper
George Kahumoku Jr
Frederick Kamaka Sr
Skyler Kamaka
Tomos Lewis
Jeff Mull
Jason Selley
Fiona Wilson
Governor David Y Ige

**Chief photographers**
Mark Kushimi
Valerie Narte

**Still life**
David Sykes

**Images**
Alamy
Wyatt Clough
David Franzen
Getty Images
Honolulu Beerworks
The Howard Hughes Corporation
Paul H Mark, HSPLS
Philip Lemoine
Ken MacIntyre
Mariko Reed
Lianne Rozzelle
Meagan Suzuki

**Illustrators**
Satoshi Hashimoto
Don Mak
Tokuma

CHAPTER EDITING

**Need to know**
*Kenji Hall*
*Tomos Lewis*

**Hotels**
*Fiona Wilson*
*Kenji Hall*

**Food and drink**
*Fiona Wilson*
*Kenji Hall*

**Retail**
*Fiona Wilson*
*Kenji Hall*

**Things we'd buy**
*Fiona Wilson*
*Kenji Hall*
*Tomos Lewis*

**Essays**
*Tomos Lewis*

**Culture**
*Fiona Wilson*
*Kenji Hall*

**Design and architecture**
*Fiona Wilson*

**Sport and fitness**
*Fiona Wilson*
*Kenji Hall*
*Tomos Lewis*

**Walks**
*Tomos Lewis*

**Beyond the city**
*Fiona Wilson*
*Kenji Hall*
*Tomos Lewis*

**Monocle**
EDITOR IN CHIEF AND CHAIRMAN
*Tyler Brûlé*
EDITOR
*Andrew Tuck*
CREATIVE DIRECTOR
*Richard Spencer Powell*

**The Monocle Travel Guide:
Honolulu**
GUIDE EDITOR
*Fiona Wilson*
ASSOCIATE GUIDE EDITOR
*Kenji Hall*
PHOTO EDITOR
*Shin Miura*

**The Monocle Travel Guide
Series**
SERIES EDITOR
*Joe Pickard*
ASSOCIATE EDITOR, BOOKS
*Amy Richardson*
RESEARCHER/WRITER
*Mikaela Aitken*
DESIGNERS
*Sam Brogan*
*Kate McInerney*
*Jay Yeo*
PHOTO EDITOR
*Renee Melides*

PRODUCTION
*Jacqueline Deacon*
*Dan Poole*
*Chloë Ashby*
*Sean McGeady*
*Sonia Zhuravlyova*

**Resources**
*Fiona Wilson*
*Kenji Hall*
*Tomos Lewis*

**Research**
Mikaela Aitken
Kanako Arai
Noor Ibrahim
Kurt Lin
Charlie Monaghan
Zayana Zulkiflee

**Special thanks**
Kathy Ball
Jennifer Binney
Justin and Leslie Cariaga
Helen Chang
Paul Fairclough
Junji Hashimoto
Ken and Yumiko Hirata
Michelle Jaime
Tokunori Kuwahara
Edward Lawrenson
Evva Lim
Brian S Linares
Andrew Mau
Kyle Reutner
Lynette Roster
Faye Sakura Rentoule
Dean and Cassy Song
Shawn Steiman
Naomi Taga
Matthew Tapia
Lisa Yamada

New

## The collection

We hope you have found the Monocle Travel Guide to Honolulu useful, inspiring and entertaining. We're confident it will help you get the most out of your visit to Hawaii. There's plenty more to get your teeth into: we have a global suite of guides with many more set to be released in coming months. Cities are fun. Let's explore.

### Buy today at all good bookshops

Or you can visit the online stores at:
*monocle.com/shop* and *shop.gestalten.com*.